Inclusion Includes Us

Other Redleaf Press Books
by Mike Huber:

*Embracing Rough-and-Tumble Play:
Teaching with the Body in Mind*

All in One Day

The Amazing Erik

Bree Finds a Friend

Evette's Invitation

Mama's Gloves

Rita and the Firefighters

Inclusion Includes Us

Building Bridges and Removing Barriers in Early Childhood Classrooms

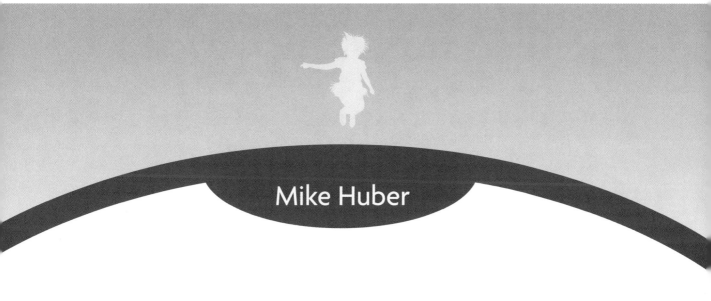

Mike Huber

Redleaf Press®
www.redleafpress.org
800-423-8309

Published by Redleaf Press
10 Yorkton Court
St. Paul, MN 55117
www.redleafpress.org

© 2023 by Mike Huber

First edition 2023

Cover design by Michelle Lee Lagerroos

Cover photograph by iStock.com/kali9; cover illustrations by Karolna/stock.adobe.com; Christos Georghiou/stock.adobe.com; Prazis Images/stock.adobe.com; frilled_dragon /stock.adobe.com; martinussumbaji/stock.adobe.com; Annie G/stock.adobe.com; Balint Radu/stock.adobe.com

Interior design by Michelle Lee Lagerroos

Typeset in Baskerville, Agenda, and New Spirit

Interior photos/illustrations by martinussumbaji/stock.adobe.com

Printed in the United States of America

Library of Congress Cataloging-in-Publication Data

Names: Huber, Mike (Early childhood educator) author.
Title: Inclusion includes us : building bridges and removing barriers in early childhood / by Mike Huber.
Description: First edition. | St. Paul, MN : Redleaf Press, [2023] | Includes bibliographical references and index. | Summary: "Inclusion Includes Us seeks to replace barriers between early childhood educators and their students with an understanding that every person in the classroom has a unique combination of needs and helping children and educators recognize the needs of others. This book will help early childhood educators reflect on how you view yourself and others in terms of both culture and abilities and offers concrete ideas for how to connect with children of all cultures and abilities and create a sense of belonging for all"-- Provided by publisher.
Identifiers: LCCN 2022018086 (print) | LCCN 2022018087 (ebook) | ISBN 9781605547756 (paperback) | ISBN 9781605547763 (ebook)
Subjects: LCSH: Inclusive education. | Early childhood educators--In-service training. | Reflective learning.
Classification: LCC LC1200 .H83 2023 (print) | LCC LC1200 (ebook) | DDC 371.9/046--dc23/eng/20220609
LC record available at https://lccn.loc.gov/2022018086
LC ebook record available at https://lccn.loc.gov/2022018087

Printed on acid-free paper

U24-03

For Remus Huber, who has taught me more about neurodiversity and gender expansiveness than any book or podcast ever could, and for Sonia Funkenbusch, who reminds me that not everything need be said.

Contents

Acknowledgments

Writing a book can seem like a solitary process, but it's only because I'm alone when I start typing. The truth is that I am snatching ideas from the whirlwind of researchers', colleagues', and students' voices that swirl in my head.

First, I want to thank the teachers, therapists, and administrators at St. David's Center for Child and Family Development for valuing collaboration while meeting difference with curiosity.

I have to thank my *Teaching with the Body in Mind* podcast cohosts Tom Bedard, Ross Thompson, and Joey Schoen, my other podcast coconspirator Heather Bernt-Santy (*That Early Childhood Nerd*) and her fellow nerds Richard Cohen, Dan Hodgins, and Carol Garboden Murray, as well as Lisa Murphy and Deb Lawrence for our porch play chats. I am grateful to all of them for our conversations where our ideas swirl together, taking on a life of their own.

My apologies to anyone who had to listen to my stream of consciousness as the ideas of this book came together when all they asked was how I was doing, especially Matt McNiff. This book would not have taken shape without Matt's tireless quest for high-quality care for all children. I owe a big thanks to Matt and Sarah Warren for reviewing an early draft and helping me organize these disparate ideas into a congruent narrative. And thanks to my editor, Melissa York, who helped me refine the text into this book.

Throughout this process, I was inspired by the knowledge and wisdom of Lyric Holmans (*Neurodivergent Rebel*), Meg Proctor

(*Two Sides of the Spectrum*), James Arthur M. (*Minority Korner*), Simon Minty and Kate Monaghan (*Ouch*), Ibram X. Kendi, Greg Santucci, and so many others who work to build bridges and remove barriers for others.

Introduction

Early in my teaching career, I was often frustrated when families brought their children to my classroom "late." I had designed the daily schedule to start with circle time at 9:00 a.m. to read the daily messages together and help children transition to our classroom and build our community. If families came later, I believed the children were "missing out." One day, Becky, who often showed up with her four-year-old daughter Lily around 10 a.m., apologized to me. I had never talked to her about being late, but my body language probably expressed my feelings. Becky told me that Lily's cystic fibrosis required her to percuss Lily's chest a few times a day, and sometimes it took longer than expected. This was my wake-up call.

The truth is, I was stuck on the idea that I was the expert of my classroom and that I was there to impart my knowledge and talents to the children. This attitude, however unintentional, does not make anyone feel included, children or their families. Of course, I was building relationships with children and families, but my expectation that families had to adapt to the culture of the program underlay everything.

There are many reasons why a family may arrive at a different time than what I ask. In this case, I realized I was so focused on what I saw as the needs of the group, I didn't think about what the daily experience of a child with cystic fibrosis was like. Once I heard the reason, I let Becky know that of course Lily's health comes first. But honestly, quietly, my first thought was "But this is how we do things in this classroom." I reflected later that week with a coteacher, and I realized that my frustration was due to a difference between my needs as the teacher—my values surrounding our start time—and the needs of the child and family. I wanted to foster a sense of community in the classroom by having circle time with all of the children. What I failed to realize at first was that creating community requires that each member feels included. This was a case of an individual need competing with the group need. Once I understood this, I realized that my insistence on all children arriving for circle time was creating a barrier that prevented this child from feeling included. I then brainstormed ways to foster community while also building a bridge that would give this child a sense of community, even if her experience was different from the other children.

Since that time, I have posted the daily schedule on the wall in visual form along with any daily messages. When a child arrives, I welcome the child and then we look at the daily schedule and read the messages together. This serves the same function as when I read the messages with the whole group. I was able to meet my goal of fostering a sense of community with families' need for a flexible arrival time.

Looking back on this incident, I can see that my assumption that the program's culture was immutable and that everyone had to assimilate to it was exclusionary. I am thankful to Becky for bringing this to my attention and so grateful that when this situation arose, almost twenty years ago, I chose to include this family and changed my attitude. I do wonder in what other ways I may have failed to notice the needs of a child or family because I did not reconsider the culture of the classroom, thinking it was simply the way things were. When I use the word *culture* in this book, I am referring to a set of beliefs, values, and behaviors shared by a group. A classroom culture is the mix of the educators' expectations for the behavior of the children and themselves and the reasons behind these expectations. Each individual brings their own culture to the classroom, so differences in beliefs, values, and behaviors—whether due to race, ethnicity, class, abilities, or any other reason—has implications for who fits into the classroom culture. Since my experience with this family, I have been interested in inclusive child care.

When I started teaching, I felt unprepared for working with children who didn't fit my classroom culture. I viewed these children as challenging, not realizing how my response to their behaviors was making my job harder. The more I tried to make the children conform to my expectations, the less they felt included. With some of these children, my stress level would rise when they arrived, or I would feel a sense of relief when I found out they would be absent that day. Throughout my career I have found ways to make my classroom culture more open to children with diverse needs, cultures, and **temperaments**. In doing so, teaching has become more joyful. I don't just tolerate the diversity of children and adults; I appreciate each person's uniqueness. For the past four years leading to writing this book, I have been coaching educators at an inclusive child care center. I help other educators learn to appreciate the differences in children's behaviors. I hope their practice becomes less stressful and more joyful as mine did. I hope that this book will do the same for you.

About This Book

This should not be the only book you read about inclusion. In fact, one main idea of this book is that if you are to create an inclusive program, you need to commit to being a lifelong learner. This book is both philosophical and practical. It will ask you to reflect on how you view yourself and others in terms of both culture and abilities as well as to reflect on how our society views diversity. At the same time, the book will give you concrete ideas for how to connect with children of all cultures and abilities and create a sense of belonging for all.

Another reason this book cannot be the only book on inclusion you read is because I can only work from the cultural perspective I bring as a white, middle-class, nondisabled cisgender man. I attempt to be inclusive of others, but I am always starting from my personal cultural lens. My ideas are constantly evolving as I learn from others with different perspectives and perform my own self-reflection. I hope this book serves as a framework to help you make decisions that include all children and adults in your classroom, but by necessity, this book does not have all the answers.

While this book has ideas that can be helpful to special education teachers and specialists, it is primarily addressing the adults who work with a set group of children daily. In most settings, this person is known as the family care provider, child care provider, or general education teacher. This is not to take away from the role a special education consultant or teacher may play, but for inclusion to be truly inclusive, the adult working with the entire community of children (and other adults) needs to take ownership for the experience of each child in the group. When one adult, usually a paraprofessional, works with the children who qualify for special education, the classroom educator often shifts focus away from these children and focuses on the children who do not qualify for special education, whether intentionally or not. Rather than bridging the experiences of children, it creates a barrier for meaningful social interaction between children who are and are not assigned a paraprofessional.

One of the central tenets of this book is that there is no straightforward differentiation between typically and atypically developing children. The term *special education* usually refers to children with learning or developmental disabilities who receive additional services in an education setting. *Special education* has legal implications in terms of the educational rights of the child under the Individuals with Disabilities Education Act (IDEA) in the United States. It has also become the term used for a distinct branch in the field of education for professionals who work with children who are covered by IDEA. *Special needs* is sometimes used to describe the needs of children who require additional support beyond what is typical in a classroom. But *special needs* can include needs not covered under IDEA, such as allergies. I have often used the phrases *typical development* and *atypical development* to discuss children who may fall outside the average in terms of child development. But when adults are not careful, the term *atypical* can become a label for a child rather than an aspect of their development, such as atypical fine-motor skills development. Another shortcoming is that what is considered *typical development* is a range, so it's not clear at what point something becomes atypical. In this book, I try to use the terms *disabled* or *disability* because there is a self-identified disability rights community that informs my thoughts. I use other terms when they are more accurate. I don't believe any single term works in every situation, and I am aware that acceptable terminology changes over time.

Each chapter covers one step for becoming a bridge-builder in your classroom, using stories from my teaching experience as well as the experiences of the teachers I currently coach. Chapter one lays the groundwork, defining inclusive child care and how it is currently practiced. Chapter two focuses on rethinking diversity, moving away from the tendency to see one culture as the norm to which other cultures or abilities are compared. Chapter three addresses self-reflection on your own culture and abilities. Chapter four rethinks our idea of who can be an expert in the field of early education. Chapter five puts all these ideas together and walks through examples to show how to use these new ideas to include all children. The words in **bold** appear in the glossary for your reference.

Including all children in our classrooms and programs starts with us realizing we bring a perspective embedded in our culture and experience. If we can recognize and acknowledge that, we can begin to appreciate the perspectives of each child and adult and give them a sense of belonging.

Identity-First Language

In this book, I primarily use identity-first language such as *disabled people* rather than *people with disabilities*. This tends to be the preferred language in the various disability communities in the United States as of the writing of this book in 2021 (L. Brown 2011; Collier 2012; Shakespeare 2018). Identity-first language is also used for specific disabilities such as *autistic child, Deaf mother,* or *blind father.* Identity-first language is also seen as more congruent with the social model of disability that this book uses (Liebowitz 2015). Disabled people are increasingly public about wanting to use identity-first language. There is a parallel drawn to race and gender. Seeing the person, not the disability, is akin to not seeing a person's skin color or gender—it is seeing only part of the person (L. Brown 2011; Collier 2012). Disability is diverse and language is always changing, so please use the language that is current for the community you are working with. Every individual will have a personal preference, and educators should use the terms that a particular child and their family uses.

Chapter One

Including Children

The terms *inclusive child care* or *inclusion* are often used to describe child care programs that have children with special needs learning alongside other children. The terms separate these programs from special education programs that serve only children with identified special needs as well as from general education programs. General education programs often simply go by terms such as *child care*, *preschool*, or *day care*. There is an assumption that these programs are the norm and other programs are—well, special. Making a distinction also loses sight of the fact that many children are not diagnosed in the first five years, so general education programs often serve children who will be labeled "special needs" later in their lives.

The terms *inclusive child care* or *inclusion* also suffer from their passivity. It makes it sound like "inclusion" is something that just happens if you put disabled and nondisabled children in the same room. But disabled children have to be intentionally included. Failure to do so means we are excluding them. This lends an immediacy to our work.

All the adults in the program—the parents, educators, and support staff—also need to be actively included for the children to thrive. I think the first step to help ensure that everyone is included is to shift your focus. Rather than focusing on *including* children with different needs, focus on finding ways to give children a sense of *belonging*. *Including* children and their families is what educators do. *Belonging* is what the children and families feel. I believe that making belonging the focus helps educators identify strategies they can put into practice.

In my experience, the current approach to inclusive child care falls short because it treats the culture of the school or program as a universal, and then some accommodations are made so the "special" child fits this culture. This is a bit like shaving the corners of a square peg to fit a round hole rather than adding a square hole so that there is more than one way to fit in. Books on inclusion often explain how to help disabled children meet the same learning goals as nondisabled children, with little focus on the relationships the children have with others. In the book *Inclusion in the Early Childhood Classroom: What Makes a Difference?* Susan Recchia and Yoon-Joo Lee point out that "the effectiveness of inclusion has been evaluated through measuring specific outcomes for children with disabilities" (2013, 4) rather than "how meaningful the social experience is to the child" (5). In other words, the child's sense of belonging is removed from the equation.

At the program where I work, at one time we used the fairly typical approach of assigning a paraprofessional to disabled children. What we found was that usually the paraprofessional became the social focal point for that child. The classroom teachers and many of the children didn't form a deep relationship with the child if a paraprofessional was involved, which meant the child was inadvertently excluded from the classroom community. We would have to be more intentional to break down the barrier between the children with a paraprofessional and those without.

We also had a second issue. Our program was located in a predominantly white suburb, and the program mostly served people in the neighborhood who paid tuition. The disabled children came through a county system, so they came from anywhere in the county. The result was that almost all the BIPOC children in our program were disabled. Most of the white toddlers' and preschoolers' only interactions with

BIPOC peers was with children who had a paraprofessional, and most of the BIPOC children's experience with white peers was at our center where they weren't quite fully part of the community. All of the children experienced racial diversity, but we needed to be more intentional about how they were experiencing it. We had to be aware that all children come to our center with the context of their family and culture. Ignoring the cultural context means ignoring who the child is.

The pandemic temporarily shut down our program, and we took time to rethink our structure as we slowly built back up. This gave us a chance to look at how we might include all children. As you are thinking about ways to include all children, it may be helpful first to understand how our field got to this point. There was a time when disabled children had very limited educational opportunities, similar to the way that non-white children had limited opportunities—and too often still do.

Including All Children

The field of special education expanded in the early 1970s with section 504 of the Rehabilitation Act of 1973 and the Individuals with Disabilities Education Act (IDEA), which passed in 1975. Before this time, most disabled children were educated in separate institutions, some of which spent little time on what we would consider teaching and learning. IDEA required that disabled children be educated in the least restrictive environment possible, giving rise to inclusive education. Often inclusive programs have teachers or specialists with a degree in special education. However, I fear that the rise in special education as a field has resulted in another segregated system where the field of general education (or simply *education*, as it is commonly referred to) doesn't address the full range of children, leaving some children for the specialists.

In early childhood education, it has been my experience that far too many educators feel unprepared to work with children whose behaviors are interpreted as challenging. I work with over a hundred educators every year as a trainer in the field. I find that at almost every training—regardless of the topic—someone will ask for advice to support a child who challenges them. Many of these challenges seem to be behaviors that are fairly typical for young children, but the classroom or family child care is not set up in a way that allows for active children or for children learning to control their emotions. Some of these children may have identifiable special needs that could result in a diagnosis, but many of the children probably do not. The caregivers asking these questions know what they are doing now isn't working, and they just want to know how to help the child.

When I was in the classroom, I found myself in similar situations. Over the years I have concluded that part of the problem is a binary thinking that views children as either "typical" or "special needs." Many children fall somewhere in between, but most preservice and in-service training I have seen still focuses on "typical" child development separately from special needs. I focus more closely on the problems I see with binary thinking in chapter two. I worry that when the adults find behaviors challenging, the child does not feel like they are fully accepted in the classroom community.

The truth is all children have needs and all children have a range of abilities. For many children, these needs and abilities fit into the way early learning programs are typically designed. But far too many children find themselves repeatedly told their behavior is unwelcome in the classroom. While occasionally a child has needs an educator is not able to address adequately, I believe the vast majority of children can be a vital part of any classroom community if educators understand how to address barriers a child may encounter and facilitate bridges between children. These strategies can be used to address what are often called challenging behaviors or to support children with a diagnosed disability.

I don't pretend the strategies in this book are effortless, but they will alleviate the frustration many feel when they are confronted with challenging behaviors. In my own experience, I felt less frustration and stress as I made these changes. When educators bring up these behaviors at one of my trainings, my answer is fundamentally the same each time: What can you do so the child feels they belong in the classroom? Rather than focus on how to make the child fit in to the classroom culture, we need to create a culture that fits all children.

Ensuring each child feels like they belong in the classroom starts with an understanding that all learning is anchored in social-emotional development. As educators we must focus on the emotional development of each child and encourage relationship building in the classroom community both among children and among children and adults. As children learn to express and regulate their emotions, they feel more emotionally secure. Children who have experienced trauma may take a while to learn these skills, but emotional security is key to them feeling a sense of belonging. When children feel emotionally secure, they tend to trust others and develop positive relationships. Fostering relationships in a group environment requires the caregiver to help children understand their differences, whether based in their personality, interests, culture, or abilities. Once again, we must acknowledge the cultural context of each child if we are to truly appreciate who they are while also recognizing our own cultural context and how that might influence our interactions with the child and family.

The more emotionally secure children feel and the more they are able to build relationships, the more they tend to explore and engage with others. When children explore and engage more, they learn more in all areas of development. This foundation of social-emotional learning is necessary for all other learning. Too often currently, inclusive classrooms focus on specific academic outcomes for special education children to determine success, often ignoring not only the social world of the group overall but even the social needs of these very same children (Recchia and Lee 2013). This is not to say that we should ignore academic outcomes for these children—but we must acknowledge that social-emotional outcomes are just as important as academic ones, especially in the early years.

I have seen many **Individualized Education Plans** (IEPs) that include a goal that says the child will sit with the group at circle time for five minutes. There are often strategies for using equipment such as a wiggle seat to allow children to shift their body weight while staying in the same spot on the floor or fidgets to use with their hands. What I have not seen listed in these IEPs are educators' plans for activities that interest this particular child or involve a wide range of movements. In other words, the only thing that has to change is the child's behavior. I wonder what would happen if a goal asked other children in the classroom to try to follow this child's ideas. Recently, I led a circle time in a classroom and children took turns choosing a movement the others would copy. One child with limited mobility mostly watched the others, raising her hand or foot slightly as a way of imitating her peers. When it was her turn, she held herself up with her arms on her walker and marched in place. The other children enthusiastically marched around. By focusing IEP goals only on strategies to have the child adapt to the classroom and not on how to adapt the classroom to the child, educators are encouraged to focus on the child as falling short rather than focusing on ways that the child can contribute to the classroom community.

I have found it beneficial to determine what helps and hinders children's sense of belonging. I have used two simultaneous processes to do this: addressing barriers and building bridges. The social model of disability helps identify and address barriers while cultural humility helps build bridges for all children and adults to be included in the classroom. I want to start by focusing on some of the barriers to inclusion and how we can remove many of them.

Addressing Barriers in the Classroom

As mentioned, before 1975 there was virtually no attempt to include disabled children in general education classrooms. When IDEA passed, many people argued that it would be impossible to implement. I think many of these people were unable to see how many of the barriers to full participation for disabled children are created by society, not their impairment. I find that a social model of disability is helpful in framing the classroom as a place of belonging. The social model views disability as a societal problem rather than an individual problem. Individuals may have impairments, but the disability comes from barriers in society (Oliver 1990; Shakespeare 2018).

Ronald, a social worker at a high school for disabled teens, told me a story that illustrates this point. He was helping Fran, a seventeen-year-old, land her first job interview. Ronald was surprised when Fran called from outside the office building before the interview.

Fran sounded desperate. "I don't think I can do this!"

Ronald encouraged her, "Of course you can. You're smart. They are looking for someone with your knowledge."

Fran was taken aback at Ronald's ignorance. "No! I mean the door has a knob. I can't open it!"

In this story Fran had the ability to do the job she was interviewing for. The disability was not Fran's—rather it was the office building that presented a barrier for her to enter the building. Fran was able. The door to the building "dis-abled" her, or more accurately, the society that allowed such knobs on doors did it. Judy Heumann, quoted in *New Directions in Special Education*, put it this way, "Disability only becomes a tragedy for me when society fails to provide the things we need to lead our lives: job opportunities or barrier free buildings" (Hehir 2005, 14).

In the world of education, we need to take a look at the learning environment, both physical and emotional, and ask, "What are the barriers preventing a child from engaging in the community?" This is a little different than figuring out "the why behind a behavior," as is sometimes suggested in inclusion literature. Instead we focus on the variables that cause problems for the child or others. You don't need to know the medical diagnosis of a child who uses a wheelchair—rather, consider whether they can access all areas and materials in the classroom. Can they get in and out of the chair themselves? Are they able to play on the floor? The same is true for mental health and **neurodivergence**.

In one of our classrooms, a child named Phil would get upset if a teacher did not verbally respond to him, even if the teacher was talking to someone else. He would often yell and knock over chairs. Phil was being assessed for mental health services. Before there was a diagnosis, his teacher Anna found through trial and error that Phil could wait if he was given a way to mark the time: "Why don't you build a truck with blocks while I finish talking to Dustin?" When Anna used this approach, Phil would smile and head over to the blocks and then come back. Anna did not need to wait for a diagnosis. His inability to wait was a barrier to Phil being included in the classroom. Anna addressed the barrier by trying different ways to approach the situation until one worked. Phil did receive a diagnosis that resulted in him working with mental health professionals, but he still was in Anna's classroom every day. This is a fairly pointed example of a child feeling excluded and an educator finding a way to include him.

Educators can intentionally address barriers that exclude children by using the social model of disability. To do this, we need to look at the different types of barriers that children or adults might encounter. Tom Shakespeare categorizes typical disabling barriers in our classrooms into three categories, related to the physical environment, to the informational environment, and to negative attitudes (Shakespeare 2018). I would add a fourth category, cultural barriers. Physical barriers refer to children having access to all materials and areas of a classroom. Informational barriers relate to children having the information needed to engage in the classroom, including language such as sign language and visual communication. Attitudinal barriers (negative attitudes) can be explicit when an educator thinks they cannot "handle" certain children, or implicit when an educator interprets behavior as defiance. Cultural barriers happen when classroom rules or expectations are based on one culture and behaviors that are typical in other cultures are misunderstood.

As we address barriers in our classrooms, it should be noted that the social model distinguishes between *disability* and *impairment* (Connor 2011). A *disability* is created by barriers in society. *Impairment* "refers to the underlying health condition" (Shakespeare 2018, 3). Impairments are typically addressed by therapists, medical personnel, specialists, and others. The general educator's role is more practical in addressing barriers that affect a child's or adult's ability to be an active part of the community. You don't need to know the specific medical condition that causes a child to need leg braces for mobility, but you do need to know whether the classroom environment is preventing the child from engaging.

The differentiation between *disability* and *impairment* has gray areas, and at times the educator does address the impairment. For example, an educator may feed a child with a feeding tube. This book is not arguing that the impairment is never an issue but instead advocates that educators can include most children in the classroom by focusing on disabling barriers first.

Physical Barriers

Physical barriers are not always obvious until a situation arises in which someone encounters a block. At a basic level, there needs to be enough room for wheelchairs or other mobility devices to maneuver. There also needs to be room for children who need movement. If a child is frequently told to "wait until they get outside" to move boisterously, the child has a need to move that is being ignored by the educators. Physical barriers can also relate to sensory issues, such as bright fluorescent lights that cause many people stress. To address these needs, educators can set up the environment so it allows children to access all areas of the room, including areas to play in groups and alone, places to play physically and places to sit, places to be messy and places to avoid messy materials, and places to be loud and places to be quiet. Even after doing all this, educators may observe a child who still is unable to fully engage in the classroom. Regular reflection, discussed in chapter three, can help address these barriers.

Here are some typical physical barriers and what they might look like in an early learning setting:

Physical Accessibility	Considerations and Solutions
Space for wheelchairs	Furniture is spaced for a wheelchair to fit. Materials can be reached by a wheelchair user. Tight corners that are hard to maneuver have been eliminated.
Materials	Materials should be accessible to all (barring choking hazards or other safety concerns). Consider storing materials in multiple locations to improve accessibility.

Physical Accessibility	Considerations and Solutions
Chairs, tables, and other furniture	All children and adults can use furniture in the classroom. Offer specific furniture as needed to accommodate individuals.
Bathroom facilities	Sinks and toilets are accessible to all. Diaper changing table and supplies are accessible to all adults.
Doors	Doors should have accessible handles or open and close automatically.
Sensory Accessibility	
Overstimulating (child avoids or moves away from sensory stimulus)	Allow a child to go under tables or in nooks to lessen sound or brightness. Allow a child to move away from a group of children who are cleaning up or engaging in an activity. Find opportunities for a child to build with blocks when others have left the area (even if others left for a group activity).
Under-stimulating (child rarely engages with materials or peers)	Encourage a child to engage with materials or peers by playing with the child or changing materials to provide something the child finds inviting.

Informational Barriers

Informational barriers are addressed by creating materials and communicating the information as needed. The educator builds a bridge between the information and the child's understanding of it.

Informational barriers in early childhood classrooms differ from classrooms for older children because none of the children can read print fluently. Materials need to be labeled in ways that children understand: a photograph, drawing, raised drawing, or the object itself fastened to the outside of the container. The materials should be organized in a consistent way so children know where to find them.

One strategy that can break down informational barriers is using visual schedules. They are a quick way for all pre-reading children to learn what they can expect each day. If a child misses their mom, a quick glance at a visual schedule reassures them that Mom picks them up after snack. Other children need visuals to help through shorter sequences such as "First clean up and then lunch." How much information a child needs is related to their ability to remember as well as how stressed they are. You may need to remind one child several times that the class will be going back inside soon, while another child will simply follow the others in.

Educators should use the home language of the child when speaking to them whenever possible. If this is not possible, educators should learn several key words from each home language used in the community. Learning the instructional language in the classroom should never happen at the expense of honoring and valuing alternate home languages. This advice is somewhat different for Deaf children because they cannot hear the educators' words to learn the language. Instead, they either need a sign language interpreter (typically American Sign Language, or ASL, here in the United States), or the educator needs to be fluent in sign language.

Here are some typical informational barriers and what an educator might do to bridge understanding for all children:

Informational Accessibility	Considerations and Solutions
Daily schedule	Make a visual daily schedule. Give verbal reminders for transitions. Plan with some children for an upcoming transition. Use home languages when possible.
Self-care tasks	Make visuals for handwashing, snow gear, etc. Make visuals for emotions. Use home languages when possible.
Classroom materials (toys, art supplies, etc.)	Apply labels that can be read by children (visual, raised picture, object). Use home languages when possible.
Background information on an experience or topic (for collaborative pretend play, book reading, etc.)	Help one child give background information to another child who needs it in collaborative play (e.g., is the character the hero or villain?). Offer background information for teacher-led activities.

Attitudinal Barriers

Teachers Karina and Natsuki had an active preschool classroom. Three children often entertained themselves by banging on a table and yelling. When Karina or Natsuki asked them to use inside voices, the children would usually run away, yelling louder.

The teachers asked me what they could do when these children got "silly." I asked if either of them had tried being silly with them. I suggested that next time the children bang on the table, one of the teachers should join them. If one of them joins them with the attitude that banging on a table and yelling can be fun, she may discover why it is so appealing to these children. At the same time, the children will see that she is on the same team as them, strengthening their relationship. The children will have a greater sense of belonging. The children will probably yell less often, and when they do, the teachers will have a new attitude.

The barrier to the children's sense of belonging was the attitude of the teachers.

I have found that attitudinal barriers can be the most difficult to address in myself because I am often unaware of my own attitudes. In my first few years of teaching, I arranged the classroom and the schedule based on what I saw other teachers do. If a child struggled in some way, I tried to help them "learn" to follow the classroom rules or procedures. These rules reflected my attitudes and my goals. Rather than being on the same team as the child, I had a competing goal. But when I adopted a different attitude, I could assume the child was an expert in what they needed and adapt the way we did things based on their needs and those of the other members of our classroom community. I think this is how we can give each child a sense of belonging.

This same problem—trying to bend the child to fit the rules—is pervasive in special education. One of the biggest drawbacks of the dominant culture of special education is that it can be "obsessively preoccupied with 'scientific' interventions aimed at 'deficits'" (Connor 2011, 2). This focus has left many general educators and caregivers feeling unprepared for dealing with students receiving special education services. I think part of the problem is that this division between general and special education has standardized the design of classrooms and family child care, both in licensing standards and in most early childhood education textbooks. One of the ways I see this affecting children is the lack of space in most classrooms for children to run, climb, or engage in other physical play. Strength, coordination, and dexterity are emerging skills. An educator can expect that children need to move around most of the day, and at times they will knock things over or hurt themselves or others unintentionally. Despite this developmental knowledge, the dominant culture of early childhood education expects young children to sit for much of the day and views unauthorized movement as negative behavior (Huber 2017).

Children who need more physical play are sometimes expelled for "behavior problems" without the educators first offering more physical play in the classroom. This affects boys more than girls because statistically, boys engage in more physical play. I witnessed a similar dynamic when I started at my program, as boys were overwhelmingly referred to for evaluation for other services. Walter Gilliam has shown that boys are expelled at four times the rate of girls, but this number goes down if a behavior specialist consults with the educator (2005). In other words, changing the classroom or the educator's behavior can affect whether a child receives special education services or indeed whether they remain in the program. In my program, when we offered more opportunities for physical play to all children, not just the child who was a concern for the teacher, most of the children engaged. The teachers in the room reported that all the children were focusing more throughout the day. The change also fostered more play among children. Changing the attitude toward movement helped in three ways: it allowed the children who needed lots of physical play to feel that their preferred type of play belonged in the classroom, other children stopped seeing these children as the ones the teacher was frequently calling out, and all of the children benefited from more physical play. I have found that educators who allow more physical play learn to appreciate what children bring to the classroom and refer fewer children for special education services.

Children need the same space and permission in the classroom to develop emotional **regulation** and relationship skills. Educators should assume that children are developing these skills and will need help. The way children build relationships will not always look the same, often due to cultural differences, temperament, or **neurodiversity**. Adults often need to serve as the bridge between children. This is especially true for disabled children, who according to some studies tend to have fewer friends in group settings compared to nondisabled children. The first step in building bridges between children is to move from binary thinking to constellation thinking, as discussed in chapter two.

Many neurodivergent children learn social-emotional skills differently than **neurotypical** children, and they often need a more intentional approach. Educators tend to approach social-emotional skills in two main ways, *regulation-based* or *compliance-based*. *Regulation-based* approaches focus on helping children regulate their emotions to engage in the classroom. Educators foster relationship-building skills as well as emotional-regulation skills that focus on labeling emotions and learning techniques to calm down when upset. *Compliance-based* approaches focus on children following classroom rules, which are essentially cultural norms. For neurodivergent children, this compliance-based approach is sometimes referred to as "social skills." It should also be noted that the "social skills training" often used in applied behavior analysis (ABA) therapy, the most common therapy used for autistic children, is viewed by many autistic adults as damaging because it focuses on learning behaviors that make neurotypical people more comfortable rather than supporting the autistic person. The techniques to change these behaviors do not allow much space for the creativity or individuality of a play-based classroom (Fincham and Fellner 2019). Rather than valuing the different abilities children have in interacting socially, compliance-based approaches reject this diversity. What is needed to include these children is an attitudinal shift in what is acceptable or normal.

The chart below has some typical attitudinal barriers and what the educator can reflect on to try to adjust their attitude:

Attitudinal Accessibility	Considerations and Solutions
Diversity in movement needs • Some children need to run frequently, have trouble sitting still, etc.	Understand some children need to move more than others for optimal development. It is not a sign of "immaturity" or "defiance" but rather a sign that the child needs to move.
Diversity in sound and volume needs • Some children are quieter and some louder when playing • Some children are affected by loud noises	Understand that some children play loudly and it is not a sign of "immaturity" or "defiance." Use a problem-solving approach if the louder play bothers other children.
Diversity in social behaviors and relationship skills	Understand that some children are ignored by peers and may need an adult to encourage or facilitate interactions.
Diversity in emotional and self-regulation skills	Understand some children frequently go into fight, flight, or freeze mode when experiencing emotions (pushing or hitting, yelling at others, inconsolable crying, withdrawing for extended time).

Cultural Barriers

While the early childhood education field has struggled to be inclusive of children with diverse abilities, it has also struggled to meet the needs of children who belong to a different culture than their teacher or provider. In the United States this has often taken the form of a white educator teaching BIPOC children. In the classroom, culture often shows up as how a person understands and moves through the world. In young children, this can present as how a child speaks and listens to adults, how they expect adults to talk to them, how they initiate play, and how they deal with social conflict. I remember when I first started teaching, I asked a group of children, "Do you want to clean up for snack?" I did not intend for this to be a question, but rather a "nice" way to tell them to clean up for snack. When they said no and kept playing, I used a stern voice, "It is time to clean up for snack." Reflecting with my director afterward, I realized that when I was growing up, my mom often told me to do things by asking a question. Culturally, I knew that it wasn't really a question and I didn't really have a choice of answers. When I communicated with these children using this cultural construction, I discovered they were used to adults speaking more directly, the way I did the second time. This miscommunication is sometimes referred to as a **cultural disconnect** because the same words have different meaning depending on the person's cultural perspective. When the children told me no, I interpreted their response as defiance and I got upset. My reaction was based on my own cultural expectations. My interpretation and reaction is sometimes referred to as **implicit bias**.

In this example, I was able to identify my bias after the fact. The more I reflect on situations like this, the more I can notice my cultural bias the next time it comes up, before acting on it. I still have the same gut feelings I did thirty years ago when I started teaching. I still feel disrespected when certain situations arise. The difference is that now when I have that feeling, I usually recognize the cultural disconnect. In a sense, I am always striving to make my implicit bias explicit.

I think most educators would say they accept cultural differences. However, we know that BIPOC children are referred to for special needs at a higher rate than white children, and the rates of suspension and expulsion are also higher for BIPOC children. Given that the vast majority of educators of young children are white and female, it seems that educators need more tools to include children from a different race than their own.

Cultural barriers require the educator to reflect on their own cultural beliefs, values, and behaviors. Sometimes the educator will find they need to adjust their own attitudes, while other times they need to bridge competing cultural expectations of children in the classroom. The chart below has some typical cultural barriers and what the educator can reflect on (discussed in greater depth in chapter three) to try to adjust their attitude.

Cultural Accessibility	Considerations and Solutions
Eye contact	Understand that eye contact is considered disrespectful in some cultures, while in other cultures it is a sign that one is paying attention. Understand that eye contact is stressful for many autistic people.
Interdependence vs. independence	Understand that some cultures value adults helping children while some value children doing things on their own.
Direct or indirect language	Understand that some cultures give commands with direct language ("Put the toys away") while other cultures give commands by asking a question ("Would you like to put the toys away?"). Understand that some cultures expect courtesy language from children ("Can I please have some water?") while other cultures expect courtesy language from all ages ("Could you please put away the toys?").
Personal space	Understand that the distance at which one person is comfortable may make another person uncomfortable.

The field of early childhood education has primarily addressed issues of race and culture with a cultural competency approach. In Minnesota, where I teach, and in many other states, licensing requires child care workers and other teachers to receive training in cultural competency. Writing in the journal *Diversity and Equality in Health and Care*, Brenda Freshman warns that the cultural competency approach teaches people to tolerate diversity rather than appreciate it because it focuses on learning about groups in the abstract rather than engaging with individuals in that group (2016). Cultural competency, as it is frequently practiced, put simply, is the notion that when working with a child whose culture differs from their own, the educator can learn about that child's culture and then provide more appropriate teaching methods for the child. If trainers are not careful, cultural competency training can also lead to the idea that a certain group is monolithic (all Black people are this way, Asian Americans are this way, and so on).

My personal experience with cultural competency training is that the sessions assume whiteness as the norm. I attended these types of trainings in my first few years of teaching. The trainings helped me realize I was unintentionally excluding children at times due to my cultural perspective. But the trainings were typically focused on me, as a white educator, learning about other cultures with little or no time spent reflecting on my own culture or considering how my cultural perspective affects the classroom rules. My classroom was racially diverse, and I was the only white person. One day I saw three Anishinaabe boys holding long rectangular blocks as if they were rifles. The rule in my classroom was "no guns," by which I meant no pretending to use a gun. I walked over to remind them of the rule, but one of them, staying in character, shushed me, explaining, "We're hunting." At that point I realized I was ignorant of their hunting tradition. Thankfully, my center was influenced by Louise Derman-Sparks' then-recent book, *Anti-Bias Curriculum: Tools for Empowering Young Children* (1989). I apologized to the children and stepped back to watch, using the opportunity to learn how they played hunting. I realized I would have to rethink my "no guns" rule. At the same time, I also had to keep in mind that the neighborhood experienced gun violence. There wasn't a simple answer, but I sensed that including these children meant I had to include their culture.

Looking back, I realize *I* was the barrier that kept these children from feeling included. Before this example, I had stopped children many times from pretending when that play involved guns. I had not thought about how they viewed their play. My ideas about how a classroom should be run were based on my own cultural perspective. Of course, I always view things from my cultural perspective. I cannot simply shed my beliefs, values, and behaviors. Instead, I can recognize that other cultural perspectives may have different beliefs, values, and behaviors. Before I can engage in this intellectual work, I need to foster authentic relationships with the children, families, and coworkers in my class-room. I cannot rely on abstract notions. If I had solely relied on the cultural competency model when interacting with the Anishinaabe chil-dren in the previous story, I would have researched the culture. I may have added stories about Anishinaabe culture or found ways to include their family members in the classroom, since cultural competency emphasizes the importance of family. All of these are positive actions, but cultural competency alone would not have led me to question the classroom rules I set up and consider how those could be experienced differently depending on a person's cultural perspective. I also might have put more emphasis on what I learned about Anishinaabe culture as a monolith rather than what these specific children have experienced. Rather, if I started with getting to know these children and families, I would have quickly learned that hunting is important to them. In this case, I mentioned the play to one of the dads that day and he told me they had participated in a ritual that past weekend. By focusing on the play and telling the parent about it, I think I showed the parent and child that their culture was welcome in the classroom. This was a step for me in prioritizing relationships and learning from intercultural interactions. Several weeks later, the family showed the class the regalia they would be wearing for an upcoming powwow. My curiosity and the family's openness led to a sense of belonging that I don't think would have been there if I relied simply on learning about Anishinaabe culture in the abstract. It required authentic relationships.

Authentic relationships require both parties to adapt to the other. In the story above, I could have simply asked the Anishinaabe families to come into the classroom to talk to us about their culture. As a teacher, I often invited family members to share their talents or skills. Over the years, parents came in to make fry bread, sew a button, demonstrate kayaking (on the sidewalk), bind a book, and many other skills. But if I had asked one of the Anishinaabe families to "talk about their culture," I think that would have sent the message that their culture is outside of the classroom culture, something we can learn about but not part of the classroom. It could also give the message that we expect the family to represent their entire culture rather than sharing their personal experience, which is embedded in their culture.

Culture is multifaceted. Simply knowing what ethnic group or groups a family belongs to does not take into account the other facets of their identity. Do they identify strongly with this ethnic group? What influence does class have on their identity? Their sexual orientation?

Authentic relationships also help disabled children feel included in a classroom. Each child's experience is unique. Knowing a diagnosis can help give an educator some guidance for including a child, but it is not enough on its own. How is a mental health diagnosis regarded by their ethnic community? Has the family been able to afford adaptive equipment so the child's physical disability doesn't socially isolate them? Authentic relationships can also help in the case of a child who has an undiagnosed need, because the family can share ideas for including their child. We need to focus on the whole child rather than respond only to the diagnoses.

Cultural Humility

Cultural competency can be a barrier to inclusion, but the related concept of cultural humility can work as a bridge. Cultural humility is a model for working between cultures that recognizes the complexity of culture. It asks educators to look at differences in culture as opportunities to learn from each other and find mutually beneficial solutions. Essentially it asks educators to share the same goal and to be on the same team as the child. Cultural humility was first proposed by Melanie Tervalon and Jann Murray-Garcia for the medical field in 1998. They wrote that cultural humility "incorporates a lifelong commitment to self-evaluation and critique" (1998, 123) and demands that "the physician relinquishes the role of *expert* to the patient" (121). It has since been applied to education (Haynes-Mendez and Engelsmeier 2020).

Cultural humility asks that educators and/or medical professionals follow these practices:

1. Value diversity. No culture is superior or inferior to another culture.

2. Understand their cultural views. Everyone has a unique, multifaceted culture that affects their perspective, beliefs, values, and behaviors.

3. Manage the dynamics of difference. When disagreements or misunderstandings occur, look for possible cultural differences.

4. Recognize the student/client as an expert in their needs.

5. Develop partnerships with individuals and groups who advocate for others. The issues are larger than one individual, so systemic change must also happen—whether in the center the educator works in or the wider community.

Early childhood education has a few features to consider when applying cultural humility. Most notably, the classroom has multiple children and often two or three adults, so educators must simultaneously assess the needs of individuals as well as of the group. Also, children generally do not articulate their needs (or strengths) verbally but rather through their behavior. It is up to the educator to observe children's behavior with the understanding that the child is the expert. In addition the family members of the child are also experts on the child.

In the following example, Jennie was trying to understand preschooler Wally better. He sometimes struggled in the classroom, getting upset at even the smallest changes. As often happens in early learning programs, there was no diagnosis to guide this. Wally was Mexican American and Jennie was white, leaving the possibility of cultural miscommunication as well. Jennie needed to consider her relationship with the family as well as her observations to decide how to best support Wally.

Overnight, a pipe had burst in Jennie's classroom. When the class was held in a different room in the community center the next day, Wally started crying and fell to the floor outside the door. Jennie could not console him, so she took him to the old classroom. Wally looked around the empty classroom and pointed out where everything had been. "Kitchen." "Group time." Jennie had her coteacher text her photos of the same areas in the new room. She showed Wally, and he soon became curious and willingly went to the new classroom.

Jennie had been noticing that Wally often struggled to engage with others in the classroom. He seemed genuinely interested in his classmates, excitedly shouting their name as they entered, but he rarely joined them when they played. Jennie also noticed that Wally got very upset when the room was loud. The intensity of his emotions made Jennie wonder whether Wally needed more support. His behavior was showing that his needs were not currently being met in the classroom. She started having conversations with the family, emphasizing all of the things she loved about Wally. She focused on how to help him join others in play. She asked them for their perspective. Soon he was diagnosed with autism and began receiving multiple services. Jennie did learn from the various specialists, but she mostly relied on Wally and his family as experts.

I want to expand the model of cultural humility to think about how we include children based on abilities. For example, how do we react when a child gets up from the lunch table and walks around, showing that they need to move? An educator using a cultural competency lens might try to get the child to sit down because they accept that their classroom rules are the way they are and don't reflect on how these might affect children with needs that are neglected under these rules. They might have a list of activities to try with the child during circle time or outside but are not trained to reflect on how the child's need to move affects their ability to sit for lunch. An educator using a cultural humility lens does not assume their classroom rules are immutable but rather approaches the situation with curiosity. They might see that the child needs movement and also know that the child will need to eat. Rather than see these as competing goals, the educator and child can decide how to meet those goals together. They might ask, "Do you want to jump on the mats for two minutes and then eat, or do you want to finish eating first?" The educator and child have opposing goals in the first example, but they are on the same team in the second example.

An expanded model of cultural humility that includes children based on abilities has the following elements:

- The classroom community is made up of individuals with unique strengths, needs, and culture, requiring educators to break from binary thinking: typical/atypical children, good/bad behavior, and students/educator.

- The educator makes a lifelong commitment to self-evaluation and critiquing:

  - their knowledge of their own needs

  - their awareness of their personal culture

  - their awareness of their implicit biases

  - their awareness of structural biases such as **racism** and **ableism**

- The expert on the needs of a child is the child. The educator learns from the child as well as other types of experts:

  - family members

  - community members (such as a cultural community or adults with the same diagnosis)

  - child development and medical experts

- When challenging behaviors arise in the classroom, the educator recognizes that it is possibly the result of competing needs or cultural disconnects. A problem-solving approach is used to resolve the issue.

Using the lens of cultural humility, an educator must identify and address cultural differences. The educator needs to be aware of their own cultural perspectives, beliefs, values, and behaviors and understand that coworkers, the children, and the families have different cultural perspectives. Cultural disconnects that might lead to miscommunication and misunderstandings are bound to come up. Using the cultural self-reflection process outlined in chapter three, the educator can work to identify their own beliefs and values. If the educator finds their expectations of children's behavior conflicting with a family's cultural perspective, they can identify strategies to bridge this disconnect.

When there are cultural disconnects between two children, simply having the teacher identify the differences in communication or expectations is often enough for preschool children to come up with solutions. They may not understand the concept of culture, but they are starting to understand that different people want different things. For example, a teacher might say, "She likes to sit close to you when she's playing, but you want a little more space. What can we do?" In this case, the educator is pointing out two different cultural concepts about personal space in a concrete way.

I should make it clear that the concept of cultural disconnects in the framework of cultural humility starts with the premise that no culture is superior to another culture. It's more nuanced than a person believing white people are superior to Black people. Cultural humility asks us to assume that no set of beliefs, values, or behaviors is superior to another. This can be harder to notice. For example, some cultures value children referring to teachers (and other adults) with an honorific such as Mr. Mike to show respect. Other cultures value a more informal relationship of child to teacher, so children refer to teachers by their first names to imply friendship. In this case, if a parent wants a teacher to use first names and the teacher expects to be called "mister," neither way is considered the correct way. Instead, the parent and teacher can talk about the reason behind their expectations and then find a compromise. One year, I had one child refer to me as Teacher Mike while the other children called me Mike. I explained that that is what their family does. I also worked in a classroom where one teacher was referred to as Miss Nicola and I was referred to as Mike. In both cases, the children and adults adapted quickly.

Cultural humility breaks away from an us-and-them approach that considers everyone who doesn't fit into the dominant culture as the "other" by acknowledging the culture of each person in the classroom. In this way it is similar to the ideas of antibias education presented in *Anti-Bias Education for Young Children and Ourselves* by Louise Derman-Sparks, Julie Olsen Edwards, and Catherine M. Goins (2020). This approach uses many of the principles of cultural humility and offers useful self-reflection prompts, and it has been hugely influential in my own practice. However, I find the book falls short when discussing abilities. It focuses on educators examining their attitudes about disability, which misses the point that we all have physical and mental abilities and needs, not just disabled people. Also, unlike ethnicity or race, disability is an experience that can affect anyone—as Tom Shakespeare points out in his book, *Disability: The Basics* (2018). Cultural humility as used in this book can address different abilities and needs in the classroom as well as culture. I explore this in more detail in chapter two when discussing diversity of abilities.

Engagement, Not Assimilation

The term *assimilation* usually refers to the process whereby people of a marginalized culture lose elements of their culture to take on elements of the dominant culture. In the classroom, I see assimilation including not just culture, but personality type, energy level, and ways of doing things. Binary thinking tends to lead to the dominant culture, in this case the educator's, expecting others to sacrifice their own ways or needs to integrate into the classroom expectations. Chapter two covers this in more detail.

The goal of an inclusive classroom is for all children to have a sense of belonging. If we become too focused on getting children to comply with our expectations, we can view children who do not follow our classroom culture as defiant or disruptive. This effort toward assimilating children to the classroom culture can end up excluding them. Instead, educators can focus on ensuring that all children are engaged as contributing members of the classroom community. When a child is engaged with peers or adults or engaged with materials, they are constructing their knowledge of the world.

Recently, I was teaching in a classroom with a nonspeaking autistic four-year-old, Maurice. Maurice often pushed other children in an attempt to interact with them. Unsurprisingly, the other children rarely played with Maurice when he did this.

One day, I tried to play with him but he was more interested in the other children, pushing and poking them. Then Maurice climbed up on a shelf (about two feet high), and lay across it, holding an action figure. He wasn't pushing others, and children started playing closer to him. I think children felt more comfortable near him since he was raised up a bit.

LaShanda, another four-year-old, told me that the children weren't allowed on the shelf. I figured that was the rule but also saw that this was the longest Maurice had played without pushing. I told LaShanda that he seemed safe up there. I picked up an action figure and brought it near Maurice. He swung his action figure and knocked mine a few feet off the shelf. I saw this as my opportunity to interact with him, so I said, "Whoah! It went all the way over to the basket." I brought it back and he knocked it off again. LaShanda was watching. I told her, "I think he likes watching the toy fly through the air." Maurice sent the toy flying again and LaShanda said, "He's really good at it! Bring me the other action figures." I gave her a basket of a dozen action figures. She set them out one by one and Maurice knocked them off. LaShanda smiled each time.

In this example, I knew that the classroom norm said that children don't sit on the shelves, but I also saw that the shelf helped Maurice define his personal space. Since he was lying across it and was relatively safe, I decided his engagement with the materials and eventually with LaShanda was more important than following the rule. Maurice was included in the classroom in a way that he hadn't been before. Because my goal is to have each child feel a sense of belonging, their engagement is a good way to gauge if everyone is included.

Engagement looks different for different children. It can mean playing in parallel, playing solo, watching others, or even daydreaming. You can gain an understanding of what engagement looks like for each child by observing them. When you notice that a child tends to do things alone, you may check in to see if they want to play with others but often realize they are fine. To support this child, simply describe what other children are doing to help bridge to the next stage if they are interested in collaborative play. Use each child's name; some children take longer to learn names than others. I have found that when a child frequently plays alone but watches others, if I intentionally narrate what others are doing while using the names of the children, that child joins the others in play in a matter of days. When I have narrated without using children's names, I have not seen the child join the others. I frequently relied on pronouns in the classroom ("Can you help her?") but realized that this habit makes it harder for some to learn the names of their peers. I have found that simply using names rather than pronouns increases the amount of collaborative play in my classroom.

A child may engage by going from one activity to another. You should notice them beginning to engage in an activity for longer periods, over time. If not, you may want to look for clues to what is preventing them from engaging longer. If they seem to be interested in something but get frustrated easily, it may help to join them in play and model play skills. If a child pokes at others, seeming to want a reaction, they may need to learn some relationship skills. The goal is to understand the child and identify skills that may help them engage in ways that interest them. In the previous example, Maurice seemed to want to play with others and eventually I helped facilitate his interaction with LaShanda in an activity he enjoyed.

When assimilation is the goal, the adults are more concerned with a child "fitting in" to the classroom. Sitting while a teacher is reading a book to the group is considered a success. Whether the child is truly engaged with the book, wondering what will happen next, and visualizing the story in their head is less important. A child getting excited by this same book and jumping up with excitement is considered disruptive or challenging behavior. Educators consider the classroom successful when children are following the expectations of the room, the cultural norms. This often excludes children like Maurice who struggle with these expectations.

Children need to engage with materials and with peers. This is primarily done through play. Play allows each child to choose what they are interested in and engage in ways they are able. In other words, they are included in play, rather than asked to participate in activities an adult has planned. As the National Association for the Education of Young Children position statement on Developmentally Appropriate Practice states, "Play . . . is the central teaching practice that facilitates young children's development and learning" (2020, 9). Play allows children choice, which ensures their engagement. It allows for children with different interests and abilities to participate (Roffman, Wanerman, and Britton 2011). It allows children to play alone, in parallel, or in collaboration with others. Dr. Stuart Brown, founder of the National Institute for Play, has said that play promotes trust (2017). People feel a sense of trust and attunement with those they play with or play near. Play allows children to express themselves. It also allows them to decide how much **sensory stimulus** is right for them. Some children are drawn to messy activities that others approach hesitantly or not at all. Some children may find certain sensory stimuli to be calming while others to be stressful. For example, some children may cover their hands in paint, others will use paintbrushes, and others will worry about getting near the paint. Allowing children to find this out on their own as part of play fosters their self-regulation (Chaves and Taylor 2021).

By its very nature, play encourages and often requires problem solving. Problem solving is integral to bringing a diverse group of children together into one community. Whether this diversity is due to culture, sensory differences, mental and physical abilities, or a combination of these, there is no prescriptive way for adults and children to interact that will work for everyone. When teachers plan most of the activities or when the activities are scripted (as with a "canned curriculum"), there is less room for variation from the children. In the end there will be children who do not engage and those whose ideas or contributions are not included. Instead, the emphasis is on children assimilating to the activities. But just because you don't plan most of the activities does not mean that you never lead an activity. Teachers are part of the classroom community just as the children are. Teachers sing, read books, introduce new materials, teach games, and more. The proportion of activities an educator leads varies from program to program, but the children should have choices within the adult-led activities, and the majority of the day should be children playing freely.

Accessibility versus Accommodations

A diversity of people inevitably causes barriers that would prevent some children or adults from fully engaging in the community. But barriers can be addressed or removed if the adults or the whole community work together to problem solve. *Accommodation* sometimes refers to changes that make environments accessible, but the term can be problematic. Accommodations in inclusive classrooms are usually thought of as adaptations created to meet the needs of a specific child. Accessibility, on the other hand, refers to the entire community of adults and children. This is an important distinction because it does not assume there is a "normal" setup for the environment and adaptations for "other" abilities or needs. Accessibility also recognizes that a change affects everyone. In the United States, curb cutouts were created on sidewalks to accommodate wheelchair users, but they are used by people pushing strollers, people with carts and hand trucks, and others. The same can be true in the classroom. Aids such as a visual schedule often help autistic children or those with ADHD or anxiety navigate their day, but all young children benefit from seeing a visual schedule as they develop a sense of time.

At times a particular person needs an accommodation. A wheelchair or eyeglasses are accommodations because these items are not shared among all children and adults even if they all use wheelchairs or eyeglasses. Some accommodations are unique to a situation, as in this story from a preschool classroom:

Every morning, Curtis, an autistic three-year-old, went to the basket of toy animals and lined up all the polar bears. This seemed to have a calming effect on him. If another child was already using a polar bear or if a child took one of the bears from the line, Curtis became upset, often inconsolable. Usually another child would bring the missing polar bears to Curtis. The teacher, Melody, brought this up at the classroom's morning meeting. "Curtis, you really like to use the polar bears, but it upsets you when others use them. And I have noticed some of you use the polar bears with the other animals from the basket. What do you think we could do?" Janelle suggested that the polar bears be kept in a separate basket with Curtis's name and his cat symbol on it (all children had a symbol that started with the same letter as their name so more children could "read" labels) so everyone would know that those animals were for Curtis. Curtis smiled and said, "Yeah!" The rest of the children quickly agreed, although a few were worried there would be fewer animals for the rest of the class. Janelle, ever the problem solver, asked Melody if she could get more toy animals from storage. Melody agreed.

Accommodations are not inherently bad, and there are times that accommodations are necessary, but adults should start with accessibility, making changes for everyone. Whether increasing accessibility or providing accommodations, the goal is removing barriers so all children and adults can participate.

At times, even after receiving accommodations, a child will still struggle to engage in the classroom. This may be a sign that a child needs more support than is available. If this is the case, it is important to partner with the family (further discussed in chapter four). Even if the child receives occupational therapy, mental health services, or similar, the educator still needs to make sure the child is fully included in the classroom. It is easy to think that once a child receives other supports, their specific "needs" go away like the flip of a switch. Over time, a child will likely engage more as they receive therapy, and the therapist may have suggestions for accommodations that help include the child in the classroom. But change happens gradually, so educators need to continue building a relationship with the child and support them in whatever ways they can. If a child is easily dysregulated when a routine changes, educators still need to plan for the child's big emotions. The child may calm down quicker or not get quite as upset, but it is unlikely that the child will ever adapt to change easily.

Attunement

Educators can identify possible barriers that prevent children from fully engaging by attuning to all the members of the classroom. **Attunement** is similar to empathy, in that one person is trying to understand what another is going through. I like the term *attunement* because it is active, like tuning an instrument. During the COVID pandemic I would greet children outside and bring them to their classroom. Each time I walked with a child, I said good morning and made small talk. Some children joined right in and responded to me. Others left extended pauses or did not answer. When this happened I stopped talking, as I sensed that conversation was not what they wanted or needed. If a quiet child suddenly started talking, I engaged them in a conversation. *Attunement* is this adjusting back and forth until the two of us seem to be *in tune*.

In the classroom, attunement is more complex than just adjusting how much you talk. It involves noticing how a child reacts to different situations. Do loud noises seem to make them stressed, or maybe excited? Do they like to have attention from the whole class, or do they like to blend in?

The less attuned to a child an educator is, the more likely the educator will find behaviors erratic, unexpected, or challenging. If you find this happening, resist the urge to avoid the child—most educators do not do this intentionally, but it can happen, especially when children have had traumatic experiences. When the educator casts judgment on a child's behavior (consciously or unconsciously), it can become a barrier to attunement. The self-reflection process in chapter three can help you recognize when this is happening. Once you realize it, make a point of spending more time with the child. This makes a stronger connection between you and the child while also helping you understand and attune to the child. You will find it easier to recognize the barriers that contribute to the child's behavior and accommodate the child. You will also find you are less stressed by the behavior you initially found challenging. Finally, the child is more likely to attune to you if you have a stronger connection (Statman-Weil 2020; Wymer, Williford, and Lhospital 2020).

Addressing the physical, informational, attitudinal, and cultural barriers in your classroom goes a long way in giving all children a sense of belonging. Building relationships with each child is the foundation of belonging. The closer the relationship, the easier to attune to the child. This is a dynamic process. As you attune to a child, you will deepen the relationship, which in turn allows you to attune more effectively. I find that this process also moves me away from simple labels about a child such as "loud" or "shy" or a diagnosis such as autism or Down syndrome. Instead, I move toward the many facets that make this child who they are, their strengths, needs, preferences, and interests. Seeing each child as a multifaceted individual means moving toward what I call *constellation thinking*.

Chapter Two

Moving from Binary Thinking to Constellation Thinking

We must break out of binary thinking if we are to remove barriers in the classroom and create bridges between community members. Binary thinking views a child as either typical or atypical, or considers a behavior either acceptable or challenging, and so on. This binary thinking is problematic, as it sets up certain behaviors, abilities, and cultures as "the norm," and any behaviors, abilities, or cultures outside of this as "the other."

The Unwritten Rules of Early Childhood Culture

Early childhood culture in the United States, whether family child care, child care centers, or pre-K programs, tends to follow unwritten rules. Like all cultural rules, they were not explicitly created, nor are they universal, but they are nonetheless ubiquitous. These rules grew out of a school culture that evolved in the early twentieth century that valued productive workers and was perpetuated by people who are attracted to this culture. Certain behaviors, abilities, and culture are considered "appropriate" or "the norm." Phrases such as "use walking feet," "use an indoor voice," and "sit crisscross applesauce" are common. All these phrases are euphemisms for commands, which could be translated as: don't run in the classroom, you can only speak at a volume the adult is comfortable with, and you must sit with your legs crossed. There is no evidence that these behaviors foster learning, and in fact there is evidence that lack of movement can interfere with learning (Huber 2017).

These unwritten rules around movement and sound are not based on the diversity of behaviors of young children but rather on the needs of the adults working with children and the cultural norms of those teachers. Teachers maintain these norms for a myriad of reasons. Some believe that it will prepare children for kindergarten. Others are simply using their own childhood or how they raise their own children as a reference for what they should expect from all children. There is often an emphasis on limited movement and uniformity, which can give the adult a sense of control. In practice, the adults must often remind the children of the expectations. When I started as a teacher, I found myself constantly "reminding" children to sit still, thinking stillness would ensure they were listening. As I worked with mentors, I learned to stop telling children how to sit or even demanding that they sit at all. I found that children participated in activities just as much. In fact, the children who needed to move more tended to engage longer when they had control over their body's movements. Looking back, I think all the commands I was giving children were an attempt to feel in control, but the more I gave these "reminders," the more I stressed I became because the children "weren't listening" to me, or more accurately, they weren't obeying my commands. When I stopped interrupting them and let them choose how to engage in activities, I was less stressed and enjoyed being with them more.

Many children find it difficult and stressful to meet these unwritten rules, and these rules become barriers to belonging. Children under six are still developing the automatic movements needed to complete basic tasks such as zipping and buttoning. Movements are automatic when they do not require conscious thought. During this developmental process, children need time to move. At first their attention will be on their actions, but gradually they can turn their attention elsewhere. Expecting a young child to sit with their legs crossed and pay attention to the educator at the same time is ineffective. The adult must choose whether sitting cross-legged or having the child engage in the activity is more important. The child cannot do both until their coordination to sit is automatic. Even then, sitting in one position causes people of any age to pay attention less. This is why adults swing their feet or doodle while paying attention. Unwritten rules around movement are for the educator's comfort, not because they contribute to classroom engagement.

When a child is not able to follow the classroom rules or is unaware of them, adults will often find themselves giving children commands or calling a child's name frequently. If you find yourself doing these things, realize this is a sign that you are not in tune with the child, and reflect on what the classroom need is. This is addressed in depth in chapter three.

Diversity of Abilities

Finley, a preschool teacher, called children over one by one to line up each day after they put on their snow gear. Finley would speak quietly to encourage the children to "listen." Four-year-old Ash was still developing the skill of focusing on one sound, so he was easily distracted by surrounding noises. Ash consistently did not hear his name when called. One day, Finley called Ash's name twice before saying, "I guess Ash isn't ready," and calling a different name. A minute later, Ash turned and saw most of the children lined up. Disappointed, he said, "When do I get a turn?" Finley told him, "I called your name, but you weren't listening."

Binary thinking is present when we consider some people as
"able-bodied" and others as "disabled." The truth is that each person
has their own combination of abilities. Some children run faster than
others, some run slower, and some cannot run at all. Some children
can hear better than others, some can hear well but are still developing
the executive function skills necessary to focus their attention on one
particular voice or sound, and others cannot hear as well or hear at all.
Putting children into boxes such as "able-bodied" or "disabled" can
mean misinterpreting a missing skill as a behavior issue rather than
recognizing part of a child's development if the skill is not related to a
diagnosed condition. In the previous story, the teacher, Finley, called
children using an over-quiet voice, thinking it would make the children
focus on her. The fact that Ash consistently does not notice when she
calls his name is a sign that he does not have the ability to filter out
other sounds to focus on her voice or he is highly interested in what his
peers are doing, making it difficult to focus on the teacher. Finley would
not have done this to a child who had a diagnosed hearing impairment.
Because there was no diagnosis, she does not consider Ash's ability but
rather focuses on what she assumes is his misbehavior.

Children's abilities and needs change over time as they develop. In
this example, Ash will most likely develop the ability to filter out extra-
neous sounds, but it's also possible that he will need therapy to gain this
skill or that he has a condition that never allows him to fully develop this
skill. What's important is that he does not have that skill now.

Thinking of children's current abilities and needs calls into question
the common view of misbehavior and compliance. Behavior is the way
a child communicates their needs. Early in my teaching career, I read
certain actions as misbehavior. When I was handing something out,
some children would impulsively call out, "I want one!" I would tell
them they had to wait, and I would usually get to those children last. I
don't know if I consciously thought that making them wait longer would
teach them to be patient or if I was unconsciously doing it out of spite.
When reflecting on these situations, I realized that each child was doing
the best they could with the abilities they had. I started to pass out
things first to the children who were less able to wait. After a few weeks,
I would see how they reacted to waiting a little bit, going second or

third. What I found is that the children were less stressed at these times and I was as well. I had to meet the children where they were, not where I wanted them to be.

Sometimes a child's behavior is more difficult to understand, as is often the case with children who have experienced trauma, neurodivergent children, or children with different cultural expectations. In these cases, an educator should focus less on compliance and consequences for the child and more on learning about the child by observing and reflecting on the behavior. Chapters three and four talk more about how an educator goes about this.

The able/disabled binary can also cause us, as educators, to focus on a child's lack of ability. Too often we think of a child as the autistic child rather than the child who likes hugs, or the Deaf child rather than the expert builder. No child should be reduced to one attribute—we must celebrate each child for the many strengths and interests they have.

Gender Binary: Limiting Everyone

All children should be allowed to play in ways and with materials that they choose. Play is freely chosen. Adults must take care not to assign gender to colors, toys, clothing, or other inanimate objects. There are no "boy clothes" or "girl colors." Only people have gender. At the same time, children may apply gender to the objects they use as they try to understand their own gender identity. If a three-year-old says, "I like trucks because I'm a boy," an educator can reply, "You like trucks. You're a boy." You don't need to point out that not all boys like trucks and there are children who like trucks who are not boys. At lunch you could ask all the children what they like to play with. This allows all the children to hear about the diversity of interests as well as the diversity of gender expression.

Culture: More Than Us and Them

Binary thinking also affects how we view culture. The culture of the educator informs the values, beliefs, and behaviors of the classroom. In a binary view, the classroom culture is assumed to be the norm and families are welcomed to join in, to assimilate to the culture of the classroom.

Culture is more than simply types of food, language, and holidays. Culture affects communication styles, approaches to decision-making, concepts of respect and independence, and many other invisible factors (Hall 1976). One way I see culture showing up is in the value of independence versus interdependence: *independence* meaning a child completes a task on their own and *interdependence* meaning the child accomplishes the task with an adult. Normative early childhood education culture values independence as, for example, children are encouraged to put on their own snow gear with educators helping only when a child is unable to do a task such as zipping a coat. In many cultures, parents show their love for the child by assisting them, in this case putting the snow gear on the child. The values of interdependence and independence are both valid, but a child's experience at home will influence how they understand the educator's behavior. For example, a child who is used to a parent assisting them with their coat each time may interpret an educator telling them it is their "job" to get dressed as the educator not caring for them.

Here is a story where educators have considered the competing cultural values:

Marty and Olga had a class of sixteen energetic preschoolers. When it was time to go outside in the winter, Marty would sit in a chair near the children and Olga put her gear on. The children knew that Marty and Olga could help whenever needed, but they were encouraged to put on what they were able. The children each had a visual prompt that showed the sequence for putting on their winter gear. Some children used the visuals and some referred to Olga and followed her example. If children asked for help, Marty and Olga offered assistance. When more than two children asked for help, they would ask if any of the other children could help their peers. Within the first week of winter weather, many children had identified another child or adult who could help them with certain tasks. Children whose cultures valued interdependence tended to ask one of the adults first. The adults maintained the attitude that they are caring for the children, smiling and joking with them, rather than thinking of this as one more obligation.

Marty and Olga are focusing on autonomy, rather than independence. Autonomy is seen in each child deciding what level of independence suits their needs, both physical and cultural. Autonomy, rather than independence, allows for cultural differences. Children from cultures that value interdependence may ask for more help, whereas children from cultures that value independence try to do something themselves but may need more time to do it on their own. Disabled children may need help from adults that others don't, but they can still be autonomous if they get to decide what they need help with.

Other cultural differences will come up in your classroom. Some of these cultural differences are discussed later in the book, but there is no way for one book to address all cultural differences. What is most important is understanding that each person in your classroom has a distinct cultural perspective, and it is important to resist the idea that your way is the correct way. Open yourself to other ways of thinking and behaving. Ask the families for more information if you're curious about how things are done at home. Attend cultural events in the community to experience interactions in a different cultural context. Otherwise children from cultures different from your own may not feel that they are understood or even recognize that they belong in the classroom community.

Moving to Constellation Thinking

We have seen how binary thinking about ability, gender, and culture creates barriers in the classroom. Shifting away from binary thinking toward constellation thinking can create bridges within the classroom community. Moving to constellation thinking means thinking of each person in the classroom as an individual with their own culture, strengths, and needs—regardless of diagnosis, age, or any other factors. This allows the classroom to become a community where everyone is a contributing member and everyone belongs.

It is easy as an educator to get stuck in thinking that the way you do or perceive things is the norm and the children must adapt to you. Slightly better is the attitude that you might make a special accommodation for a child but still hold the norms for everyone else. But the way you do things and perceive things is simply your culture. You have a choice to shape the classroom culture so it mirrors your own or to help it evolve to include multiple cultures and perspectives.

I borrowed the term *constellation* from a collective of educators and therapists known as Gender Justice in Early Childhood, as described in their book, *Supporting Gender Diversity in Early Childhood Classrooms* (Pastel et al. 2019). The authors use a constellation model to recognize the many disparate elements that make up a person's gender, including self-identity, legal assignation, anatomy, physiology, clothing, hairstyle, speech patterns, pronouns, activities, and more. Traditional views on gender simply box all these elements into two categories, male or female. Clothing, toys, colors, and other characteristics are then put into those same two categories, such as pink for girls. This view excludes anyone who does not fit into this gender binary, whether due to anatomy and physiology (intersex), identity (trans), or expression (gender nonconforming). The gender justice constellation model also recognizes the intersection of other identities and characteristics, such as culture, income, and ability. Each characteristic is one star in the constellation that makes up the child's identity.

This idea of a constellation of multiple people with multiple identities can feel overwhelming. What I like about the constellation analogy is that you don't need to focus on all the "stars"—the points of identity—at once, but rather only on the points that you need for your current reflections. This is analogous to filtering out the other stars to only see the constellation Orion. In the classroom, different aspects of a child's identity become more relevant at different times. For example, if a child does not celebrate birthdays for religious reasons, you are focusing on the child's religious identity.

With constellation thinking, you still have a structure for how your classroom is run, but when you find that the way you have been doing things runs up against a child's cultural, emotional, or physical need, you adapt. In this example, Ross focuses on a child's gender:

Ross, a family care provider, reflected on his use of the term "boys and girls" when he calls children over. He thought about the perceived gender of each child in his class. As far as he knew, all the children identified as either a boy or a girl, but he had been reading that gender identity is primarily developed in the first four years of life. Ross had also noticed Nick, a four-year-old, often taking on roles such as mom, princess, and Dorothy from the Wizard of Oz. While Ross did not know if Nick was exploring gender identity or just taking on roles that seem fun, he did worry that using the term "boys and girls" so often may make Nick feel excluded.

Ross realized he could just as easily say, "Hey everyone, lunch is ready," and it would serve the same purpose without potentially creating a barrier for someone. He didn't need to know if this helped Nick specifically, but he knew that he valued inclusion, and this small change could be a bridge to belonging for someone now or in the future.

Constellation thinking recognizes differences as a positive thing. Children notice differences and sort things into categories. This includes people. Children notice physical characteristics as well as behaviors, while adults often get uncomfortable and change the subject. This silence sends a message that the differences children notice are "bad" or "wrong." It reinforces that there is one culture and one way bodies look or behave, in the binary of *us* and *them*. Rather, differences are something to notice and should be part of the conversation with children. It takes practice, but I have found that starting sentences with "some" or "most" people is a simple way to get out of this binary. "Most people have two legs," "Some children like pink," "Some people with black hair speak Spanish," and so on.

Constellation of Strengths

As you normalize talking about differences in your classroom, a place to start is with differences in strengths and interests. All children and adults in a community have strengths and interests that make the group richer. Too often, adults think of a disabled child by what they cannot do rather than what they can. When we take the time, we can appreciate the creativity, artistry, athleticism, humor, and caring each individual brings. Consider the child who turns a stack of blocks into a museum or climbs a tree or helps a peer cut tape for their collaborative cereal-box sculpture. An inclusive classroom intentionally celebrates the gifts that everyone brings to the community. Think about how Jared is good at puzzles and Angie is good at drawing, rather than fixating on how Jared is usually unsuccessful at joining others in play or how Angie cannot walk.

Disabilities related to mental health often are less obvious, showing up mostly in behaviors that adults find challenging. It is easy to focus on these behaviors and define the child by them: "the aggressive child," "the attention seeker," and so on. The educator might not say this out loud, but the attitude shows up in how they interact with the child. Even with the best intentions, all of us fall into this pattern of thinking at times. Instead, focus on the strengths of the child. What do they like to do? What do they contribute to the classroom community? This can help adults as well as the other children focus on the child in a positive way. When thinking of a child's strengths, take the child's perspective. Some strengths may push your buttons as an educator. For example, a child who says "poop" at any chance might make you uncomfortable, but from the child's perspective, it's great because they have found a way to make peers laugh.

Often when we feel stressed about a child's behavior we say they are "looking for attention." If we adjust our framing to say this child is "looking for connection," we can view this same behavior in a new light. Children who are struggling are often seeking connection using the tools they have. We can help children in these situations by intentionally connecting more with them. If there is a child you struggle to connect with, resist the inclination to avoid the child. Instead, think of a few strengths. Author and child development expert Sara E. Langworthy recommends listing five strengths and then looking for those five strengths every day (2015).

It is important to note that the normative culture of early childhood programs tends to encourage some strengths more than others. For example, most adults and children give priority to verbal children. If an adult asks a group of children to choose a book to read, the educator usually listens to the more talkative child. This also happens when children are interacting without an adult. One of the roles of the adult is to help children who are less verbal be understood and included. This is about more than slowing children down so others can express themselves. It's about valuing other ways of doing things and guiding children to do the same.

The class sat together, taking turns tapping their hands as they sang. For each verse, a different child chose how to keep the beat. When it was Minna's turn, they tapped their legs to the beat. The other adults and most of the children tapped their legs and sang together. At the end of the verse, Cleve took a turn. He clapped his hands together almost inaudibly. Minna said, "He's not clapping. I don't hear anything." Practically in a whisper, teacher Mike told the class, "Sometimes we have to listen closely to hear people." The whole class quieted down. Minna exclaimed, "He *is* clapping!"

The adult can build a bridge between children, shining a light on each child by encouraging their strengths and articulating those strengths to the others in the classroom. A morning meeting is a good time to do this, gathering and talking about the day with all the adults and children. This can be done throughout the day too. When a child asks an adult for help, whenever possible the adult should direct the child to a peer who can help. The adult can also let a child know when they notice a peer showing a similar interest.

Another strategy that has been shown to help children befriend others who seem different is play partnering, often referred to as peer modeling. The idea is to have two children play together, often a disabled child and nondisabled child (with the nondisabled child modeling play skills). With a humility lens, I think of this as *partnering*, where both children learn about the other. As mentioned earlier, studies show that disabled children have fewer friends than nondisabled children. Play partnering can increase peer interactions for disabled children (White 2021).

Play partnering may seem a little more forced or coercive than is typical in a play-based situation. In my experience, it helps to assign partners for a certain part of the day. For example, in a full-day program it could be between lunch and nap. I have also seen a classroom start free play with partners and strongly encourage at least fifteen minutes of partnered play and then let the play flow naturally. After a few weeks, the children tend to choose each other as play partners at other times of the day. Inclusion specialist Kari White describes trying to match up children who share some similar interests but might not connect without encouragement, possibly due to differences in social skills or other differences the children perceive (2021).

Constellation of Needs and Preferences

Of course, thinking only of strengths isn't enough to include all children. When using constellation thinking, just as we keep in mind the strengths of everyone in the class, we also need to consider their needs and preferences, regardless of ability.

Everyone has individual amounts of sensory input and needs that they require to keep their body in a well-regulated state and their own ways of adjusting when needed. We also have individual sensory preferences. Together these make up what we refer to as a **sensory profile**. Sensory preferences also describe what activities an individual is drawn to. For example, one adult prefers to do work with their hands that can get messy, such as baking, fixing cars, or painting, while another likes doing puzzles, collecting trading cards, or knitting. One person finds that background music helps them focus while another person performs best in silence.

A person's sensory profile is tied to regulation. Regulation is having the right energy or arousal level for the situation. When I am playing with children in the classroom, I should be active and socially engaged. When I am trying to go to sleep at the end of the day, I want to be calm with a still body. I want to be somewhere in between those two states when I am driving. I am generally able to regulate according to my situation, although not always. Over time I have discovered what works for me to be appropriately regulated. For example, if I need to leave an animated discussion to go help a classroom during rest time, before joining the room I take a few deep breaths. I drink an extra cup of coffee when I am in meetings all morning. Every individual needs their own strategies to stay regulated in various situations.

My mental state also affects my ability to regulate. If I am stressed about a health concern or even just a poor night's sleep, I have less tolerance for sensory input. Loud noises and bright lights may bother me in these times when they would not otherwise. If I am aware of my stress level, I can try to counteract these effects. Movement can help calm me down, so on those days I might play chase on the playground for most of our time outside rather than just a few minutes. Inside, I might tell stories that get us up and moving like different animals.

Having an unfulfilled need makes it difficult or impossible to interact with others or materials. In contrast, a preference is the way a person likes to do something, maybe because it is easiest or because it feels the most calming or grounding. Preferences can also be based on familiarity due to cultural or family practices. When you are not able to do things the way you like, it causes stress. In general, this stress is minor and temporary, and it is healthy and can build resilience. Therefore, adults should encourage children to sometimes go outside of their comfort zone. Of course, adults should also go out of their comfort zones. On the other hand, if a child's cultural or familial preferences are repeatedly met with indifference, or worse, resistance, this minor stress can become chronic, which has mental and physical health implications.

When a need is not met, the level of stress can cause **dysregulation**. Dysregulation can be thought of as an imbalance in the body, when a child has difficulty managing and adapting to stimuli in their environment. It can often result in a fight/flight/freeze response, and it is difficult then for a person to be rational (Perry 2020). In addition, if the sensory input that causes dysregulation is consistent, it can cause chronic stress. A child who has experienced adverse childhood experiences (ACEs), such as neglect or exposure to violence, may become dysregulated more often than other children. Chapter five outlines proactive steps to decrease dysregulation or prevent it from happening as well as what to do when dysregulation does happen. The steps an adult takes are the same regardless of why dysregulation occurs, but it can be harder for the adult to stay regulated themselves when these episodes are frequent.

It is also important to notice how the teacher's preferences create implicit biases when these preferences become their lens for viewing others. For example, a teacher who prefers to sit down and read or draw may view roughhousing, which is physical and often loud, as inappropriate. The fact that the vast majority of care providers and teachers in the United States are white, middle-class women has set the unwritten rules of early childhood education to follow certain biases, for example seeing reading and writing and relatively quiet play as "learning" times and physical and louder play as "getting out their energy," even for preschoolers. Self-reflection and awareness of these implicit biases can minimize their impact, as discussed in chapter three.

The need or preference isn't always obvious, so it is important to be attuned to the child.

Sarah, a preschool teacher, liked to take her class on neighborhood walks. A few of the children were recent immigrants from Somalia. When a dog barked, these children would become terrified and stop walking. Sarah was unsure why they were reacting this way but could see the children were distressed. She turned her class around and walked a different way. Later she asked the parents of one of the children and learned that in the city these children came from, the only dogs were wild and could be dangerous.

Sarah did not know at first whether their behavior indicated a sensory need or had a cultural reason, but she was attuned to the children and knew that they were getting dysregulated so she changed routes. Later, she relied on the family as experts to increase her understanding of the situation.

The reactions young children have to sound or other sensory input can vary greatly. Children's sensory profiles are still developing and typically do not fully develop until late childhood or even adolescence. They are still discovering what makes things exciting and what is overwhelming. Occupational therapists typically expect children to have a more stable sensory profile around the age of six, although it can still vary throughout our lifetimes. Occupational therapist Megan Applewick points out that young children are still becoming aware of their sensory profile (2021). They are still discovering how much sensory input is enough to keep them engaged at a "just right" level in an activity and how much can be overwhelming. They are also learning to *modulate* and *adapt* to sensory stimuli. How much is too much? What can I do when I get overwhelmed?

Multiple exposures to stimulus can help children figure out what works for them. For example, consider a child who does not want to use finger paint. At first, they may watch others use it the first few times. Then maybe they will use a stick or brush before finally using their hands. In contrast, another child will dive right in to finger paint, cover their arms in it, and then start crying because they discover it is overwhelming. Young children tend not to notice something is too much until they are overwhelmed. Think about a four-year-old who gets very excited at their birthday party. All the guests, the activities, and the treats can be joyful one minute and then too much the next. An adult can tune into cues that the child is beginning to become dysregulated and initiate **co-regulation** strategies. "There are a lot of people and it's loud. You're crying. You seem sad. Let's go together where it's quieter to calm down." As the caregiver is attuned to the cues that child is offering, the child is reassured and in relationship with the caregiver in a consistent and predictable way over time, therefore creating a positive co-regulation experience to support the path to self-regulation. More co-regulation strategies are covered in chapter five.

All young children get overwhelmed by sensory stimuli at times, but neurodivergent children tend to do this more often. This is a combination of the way neurodivergent children process sensory information and the environments they find themselves in—which are mostly created by and for neurotypical people. This includes our classrooms. While we cannot control how a child processes sensory information, we can make our rooms more sensory aware. Here is a very basic overview of the seven senses and how they typically affect the classroom:

Sense	Things that can cause stress	What to do
Auditory system (hearing)	Some children have trouble filtering out environmental sounds (fans, motors, buzzing lights, music, background chatter), so human speech is hard to attend to.	• Move close to speak to a child. • Make blanket forts to absorb sound. • Provide sound-canceling headphones. • Use nonverbal cues with speech (point to the sink when you ask them to wash their hands). • Use ASL or a few basic signs.
Visual system (seeing)	Some children become overwhelmed by lots of visual information, bright lights, and fast-moving things.	• Hang fewer pictures and signs on walls. • Provide places to go to block out visuals (under a table, in a tent). • Include slow-moving things (fish tank, glitter jar).
Tactile system (feeling)	While some children find the following actions comforting, others can be stressed: • Hugs • Deep pressure • Light touch (e.g., brushed by peer as they walk by, feeling of clothing)	• Be aware of each child's preferences and needs with touch. • Let the class know about each child's needs when necessary.

Sense	Things that can cause stress	What to do
Oral system (taste and smell)	Children with a hypersensitive sense of smell may be dysregulated by odors that adults don't notice.	• If a child complains of a smell, believe them and air out the room if necessary.
Proprioceptive system (general awareness of the body, including the position of our body parts and their relationship to each other)	Children who bump into things, including peers, or break pencils and crayons pushing too hard may be dysregulated.	• Provide a sensory table and fidgets. • Have children carry chairs to the table or do other heavy work. • Allow roughhousing.
Vestibular system (balance, awareness of body's movement, and attention and focus)	Children who have difficulty maintaining attention or who fall out of chairs may be dysregulated.	• Provide seating or play experiences that feature swinging and rocking motions. • Allow roughhousing.
Interoception system (detecting internal needs such as hunger and bowels and bladder)	Children who have bathroom accidents or neglect to drink water may be dysregulated. Being expected to finish their food when feeling full* can cause stress.	• Allow children to use the bathroom when they feel the need (if they are able to sense this). If they can't, have them try to use the bathroom regularly. • Allow a child to stop eating when they feel full*. • Call attention to how they are feeling.

Mike Huber and Liz Nelson, "Developing Our Sensory Systems through Exploration," 2021.

*It is important to note that people hold different cultural expectations around food. If it is of value to a family that the child eats all the food given to them, you can vary the amount of food you give the child from what their peers receive. As always with cultural disconnects, there is no one correct way, but you should discuss the cultural expectation and the goal of developing the child's interoception with the family to find a compromise.

If a child still gets overwhelmed frequently after you have made these changes, an occupational therapist might be able to help. Your role as the educator is to let the parent know what you observe and suggest they talk to the child's doctor or clinic. Your role is not to diagnose but rather to give support to the child so they can engage in the classroom.

Mapping Strengths, Needs, and Preferences

A classroom community contains a constellation of strengths, needs, and preferences. Observe, and you will see patterns emerge. Children who like to paint usually like other messy activities. Some may spend more time painting their hands and arms than they do making a picture. Children who share this interest in messy play often gravitate toward each other. Other children prefer building with blocks and other materials that are not messy.

Mapping out these strengths, needs, and preferences can help you identify barriers in your classroom as well as opportunities for building bridges. This is discussed in chapter three as part of reflection, and a template is provided on pages 69 and 71 and available via QR code to use with your own class.

As you map out a constellation of strengths, preferences, and needs, you will also identify potential conflicts. For example, some children get loud when they play and others like it to be relatively quiet. I think in navigating these types of conflicts it is helpful to focus on classroom **guidelines** rather than rules. Rules are focused on what children are not allowed to do and tend to be specific, such as *no running*. Guidelines are worded positively and are more general. At my program, classrooms use two guidelines: "we take care of each other," and "we solve problems together." So if a child runs in the room, the teacher can ask the child if there is a place to run that would be safe and not interrupt others. In my classroom, I encourage children to find a spot where no one else is playing, move any toys that are on the ground, and then run in that spot.

The second guideline, "we solve problems together," views conflict as an opportunity to help children negotiate solutions, including when the educator's needs differ from a child's. Early childhood consultant and conflict resolution specialist Betsy Evans (2016; 2000) created a six-step conflict resolution process that I have used successfully in my classroom:

1. Approach calmly, stopping any hurtful actions.

2. Acknowledge children's feelings.

3. Gather information from all parties.

4. Restate the problem with both perspectives.

5. Ask for ideas for solutions and choose one together.

6. Be prepared to give follow-up support.

These six steps allow children to identify their feelings, express their concerns, and listen to the viewpoints of others. It is a useful tool for creating bridges between individuals from what otherwise could be a barrier.

Sometimes conflicting needs or preferences revolve around sensory stimulus such as lighting, bright colors, proximity to others, the volume of the room, and so on. Children will most likely not verbalize when these elements become a problem. Even with your best efforts, problems will still arise, but you can arrange the classroom environment to allow for a variety of needs. Using the previous conflict resolution model can be helpful, but keep in mind that you also have your own biases about sensory stimulus. If one child expresses joy with a loud laugh, it may bother another child, but try not to insert your *own* bias for quiet voices. Also keep in mind that you may need to articulate the children's competing needs. This is why it is helpful to normalize discussing differences, so even when children are emotionally heightened from a conflict they can understand that their needs are different from others' needs. Here is what it might sound like:

"She gets loud when she is having fun, but you don't like things to get loud near you, so what can we do?"

"He gets uncomfortable when all the lights are on, so he likes to play under the table."

"That's her way of saying 'hello.' She touches you gently. You don't like being touched on your face. Should we ask her to touch you somewhere else? Would it be okay if she touched your shoulder?"

"Seng, you're mad that his oxygen tube knocked over your building. Jack needs the oxygen tube to help him breathe and he was going to get more blocks. Jack, Seng doesn't want his block building to get knocked over. What can we do so Jack can get blocks and Seng's building doesn't get knocked over?"

These statements must be used along with the conflict resolution process. Making these comments in a vacuum won't magically make the conflict go away.

Of course, there are times when certain needs become paramount, such as nap, when the children need to rest. Using loud voices or running at this time would not be taking care of the children who are resting. Guidelines are flexible in these situations, in ways that rules are not, making it easier to include more behaviors and temperaments.

Having diverse strengths, preferences, and needs makes a community vibrant. The conflicts that arise due to these differences do not take away from this but rather strengthen the community as everyone learns to include others. The same is true for culture.

Constellations of Culture

As mentioned, everyone's values, behaviors, and ways of understanding are influenced by culture. Culture affects everything we do—and yet it is so nuanced there is no way to understand all aspects of a person's culture. The goal is not to learn everything about the culture of each child you care for. Rather it is to be aware of culture whenever planning an activity or choosing a material.

The first thing to think about when choosing materials or furnishings is the idea of "mirrors, windows, and sliding glass doors," first proposed by Rudine Sims Bishop (1990). Every person in the classroom should have "a mirror," something that reflects an aspect of who they are. Every person should also have "windows," objects or pictures that represent different cultures. Mirrors and windows can be in books, pictures, the food served, and toys as well as conversations during the day.

Bishop uses the term "sliding glass doors" for books because children can enter worlds different from their own experience. They act like windows to another culture but are more immersive. Usually if you have a few "mirrors" for each child, those same materials serve as "windows" for someone else.

Request photos of all of the families to display, and ask each family to fill out surveys to find out more about them. Tell them you want to support their family's culture because it is an important part of who the child is. You can ask what traditions they have and what their family likes to do together. Use online images to supplement the family photos that show some of the same activities from the survey. Include images of families with the same skin, eye, and hair color. Do the same for family structure—single-parent families, two-mom families, and so forth. If children have a visible accommodation such as using a walker or wheel-chair, find images of other children playing using the same devices. When thinking of mirrors of representation for the children and adults in the classroom, you will notice that certain identities are ubiquitous in books, puzzles, and other materials: white skin, nondisabled, opposite-gender parents, middle-class, car-owning, English-speaking, and so forth. You will have to be intentional about seeking representations for identities that are marginalized in our culture. It is important to note that culture is multifaceted, and each representation will not match any single child but rather a facet of that child. A Chinese American child with two moms who uses a walker should see a representation of his skin color, family structure, and adaptive equipment, but not necessarily in the same picture. More than one picture for each cultural facet (skin color, family structure, disability, and so forth) is important, so no single picture is supposed to represent an entire group of people.

Once you are assured that all children have mirrors representing a few elements of their identity, you can add other "windows" and "slid-ing glass doors" to show diversity in skin color, ethnicity, abilities, family structure, ages, genders, and other identities that aren't represented by the children in the classroom. This is especially important for young children because they are egocentric thinkers with little experience outside of their family or immediate community. Representations of diversity give them experiences they may not otherwise have. Here are some ways to do this:

- books
- dolls
- figurines
- puzzles
- photo collages based on a theme:
  - children at play
  - what grown-ups do all day
  - many types of homes

Windows, mirrors, and sliding glass doors are effective only if adults use them as starting points for conversations or engage when children start the conversation. For example, a book about a child and their *abuela* may start a conversation about the different words the children use for their grandparents. An adult can continue this conversation informally later at snack or lunch. Another way to get conversations started is to point out the skin colors and abilities of the characters in the books you read. This should not take over from the flow of the story but rather in the same way the reader makes small asides to discuss other details in illustrations. This sends a clear message that the diversity of skin color and abilities are things the class can talk about. Here is what it looked like in my classroom.

Early in the school year, I read a book about the diversity of skin colors. After reading the book, the children and I drew self-portraits using mirrors and skin-tone markers. We matched the eight different skin colors to the color of children's skin and hair using the names on the marker (mahogany, terra cotta, beige, and so forth). After this activity I used the same words when reading books.

Showing the cover of *Yo! Yes?* by Chris Raschka, I said, "This book is about two children [pointing]. This child has a white shirt with a red dot, striped shorts, mahogany skin, and short black hair. This child has a green jacket, brown pants, beige skin, and short sienna hair. I wonder what they are going to do. Let's read the book and find out."

Showing the first page of *The Paper Bag Princess* by Robert Munsch, I said, "I see two people in this picture. They're both wearing white. He has a white shirt and she has a white dress. They both have beige skin and blonde hair, and they're both wearing crowns. No one is wearing a paper bag like on the cover. I wonder what is going to happen. Let's read the book and find out."

In both cases, I read the rest of the book without stopping to comment on the illustrations unless the children brought it up. In doing this, I was showing that skin color is something that can be discussed and not just when there are nonwhite characters in the book. I read some books that are specifically about diversity, but most of the books I choose have diverse characters but do not focus on race directly.

Books should also be used in a similar way in regard to abilities. Currently, very few picture books have disabled characters, and most books about disability have a story that focuses on the disability rather than the disability being incidental to the story. These books should still be read, of course, but in addition, I think it is important to point out what is missing from the books. The conversation could go like this: "I noticed that none of the characters in our books wear AFO [ankle-foot orthosis] braces like Dexter. That doesn't seem fair to me. I was thinking we could write to the people who make these books and ask them to have more characters who wear braces. Are there any other kinds of people who aren't in these books?"

Making sure each child sees their culture represented, as well as seeing representations of other cultures, is important groundwork for the classroom. But it is just a start. Even in the most inclusive classrooms, cultural differences will still lead to misunderstandings and even conflicts. The guidelines "we take care of each other" and "we solve

Books and Diversity: Sliding Glass Doors

When using books as sliding glass doors, a collection of books should be diverse in multiple ways. The diversity is in the combination of books. Provide a mix of fiction and nonfiction covering a variety of topics. Some books should have illustrations with anthropomorphic animals and some with illustrations of people. In either case, the books should feature a balance of male and female protagonists.

The books with illustrations of humans should depict people of diverse races and abilities. However, a vast majority of the books (at least 80 percent) with diverse characters shouldn't have race, ability, gender expression, or other identity as the *conflict* in the story (for example, a Black child excluded, worry about a sibling with Down syndrome, or a boy wearing a dress). There is nothing wrong with these storylines themselves, but children should not have to see their race or disability depicted as a problem or tragedy, nor should others only see BIPOC or disabled people in this light. The cultural identity can be the focus of the story, but it should portray it as a part of the character's family life rather than something unusual (for example, having family coming over for Chinese New Year). In the books that do address an aspect of identity as the source of a conflict, it should be clear that the identity itself is not the problem but rather the way others treat someone because of their identity.

problems together" are crucial for the cycle of rupture and repair, or fight and make up, that builds authentic relationships. We all make mistakes, but if there is an atmosphere of trust, we can repair our relationships and deepen our trust in each other.

Cultural disconnects will always happen. Each of us is so embedded in our own culture that there are times when we don't recognize the cultural expectations that we have of others. I started this chapter discussing the unwritten rules of early childhood culture. Those unwritten rules are expectations primarily based on the culture of white middle-class women in the United States. The closer you identify with these cultures, the more likely you are to follow these expectations, these unwritten rules. Looking at differences as stars in a constellation rather than as two choices, the right way and the wrong way, can help us remain curious when we see a child or an adult do something differently.

I brought my class of almost all white children to a puppet show. I sat with them on the floor as we waited for the show to start. I talked to them about what the show might be like. Another preschool class showed up. The teachers and children were all Black. The children sat on the floor next to us. The teachers sat on chairs to the side. My first reaction was that the teachers were ignoring the children. Then one of the teachers called out to one of the children, "Jeffrey, lead us in a song." Jeffrey started to sing and his whole class joined in. After the first song, he led another song. Soon, my class sang along.

I sat and appreciated how there are limitless ways to work with children. It also made me realize some of my own cultural expectations for working with them. I had thought initially that the teachers were ignoring the children, but I quickly realized they were trusting the children. I realized that these children and adults were following the cultural practice of song leading, common in many Black churches where one choir member starts singing a song and others join in rather than relying on a conductor. I could appreciate this difference but knew that I could not do the same thing. If I worked at Jeffrey's center I could let the children and adults know that I had never experienced song leading before. I could ask them to show me, but it is unlikely I would start leading songs. Appreciating diversity does not mean taking on the cultural practices of others. It is approaching difference with curiosity.

Constellation thinking moves me past understanding the world as if my experience is generally universal while trivializing other experiences. An important step in breaking out of this view is to understand that your perspective is born out of your culture and not simply the way things are. I started to see my experience as one of many. Self-reflection was the first step in this discovery.

Chapter Three

Reflective Practice and Self-Awareness

Inclusion is not a simple recipe to follow but rather a change in attitude. It requires addressing barriers as you find them and recognizing when and how to build bridges. This requires reflective practice. Reflective practice is ongoing because your classroom community is always changing.

What surprised me most as I started using reflection in my own teaching is how much of the practice is *self*-reflection, not because I am always changing but because teaching is based on relationships and emotions. I can know that a child has experienced trauma and will be testing our relationship, trying to make me mad because it is an emotion they are familiar with from adults. However, keeping this in mind while the child tries to run away from the group when we are outside is different. I rely on self-talk at these times, repeating to myself, "They want me to keep them safe. They want me to keep them safe." Ongoing self-reflection allows me to do this, identifying my emotional responses to situations as well as identifying my own strengths, needs, and cultural expectations and how I can manage my emotional responses.

Understanding Strengths

Self-reflection is emotionally difficult. It can feel like you are simply pointing out your flaws, so it is important to also reflect on your strengths. In the following example from my experiences as a coach, we start with focusing on what the teacher did well and then critique actions that could be improved.

Marty, a teacher I had been coaching, entered the room. She looked nervous. She told me that she hates watching herself on video. I acknowledged that it is awkward, and I appreciated that she was willing to do it anyway. I reminded her that her goal was to label children's emotions and describe how that emotion was showing up in their body. I asked her to make a note each time she heard herself do this. I showed a few short video clips. She noticed herself telling a child, "I see you crying. You seem sad." She told another child, "You're excited. You're grabbing the book from me to get a closer look." After we finished, she was pleasantly surprised how often she used this strategy now without thinking about it. We watched the clips a second time, and she noticed a few times when she named the emotion without describing the child's physical response. She felt that she may have even mislabeled an emotion. She left the coaching session feeling good about her teaching skills while also knowing what she should keep practicing.

Marty focused on her strengths first and then found examples where she fell short of her goal. Because she started with her strengths, she knew that she was able to demonstrate the skill but had to strive for consistency.

Knowing your strengths can help you leverage those strengths to connect with the children in your classroom. If children flock around you when you sing a song, you know that when the classroom feels a little too chaotic, you can sing a song and most of the children will join you. This may be enough to reset the classroom, as children who were getting into conflicts begin singing together instead. If you have a coteacher, they will have different strengths, so together you have more ways to connect with the children.

Some people have a hard time identifying strengths because they have feelings of shame or guilt in openly acknowledging them due to cultural expectations or negative experiences in the past. Others might downplay their talents to avoid bragging or because they feel that anyone could do what they do. My experience in hiring teachers has been that even in a job interview, many will preface statements of their strengths with phrases such as "not to toot my own horn." If you find yourself having trouble, ask a few adults (coteachers, parents of the children you work with, and so forth) to say what they like about your teaching. You can also pay attention to what children ask you to do. Or you can think about what activities you do that draw children to you. Do children join you when you take on a pretend role? Perhaps children tend to come to you when they are sad. Most educators can identify several strengths once they start thinking about it. I often hear educators downplay these strengths, saying things like "Well, all teachers comfort children," or "I'm not a good singer, but the children don't know any better." Recognizing a strength isn't claiming that you are the greatest singer. Teaching is not a competition but an art—the art of connecting with children. Learn to appreciate the ways you connect.

Use these questions to help you identify your own strengths:

- What activities do children ask you to do with them? (for example, play chase, sing songs, read books)

- During free play, what activity do children often join you in doing? (for example, pretend play, drawing)

- What do parents, teachers, or other adults ask you for advice about? (for example, helping a child who is sad or mad, toilet training)

- What types of adult-child interactions energize you? (for example, hugs, pretending, singing)

www.redleafpress.org
/iiu/qr-1.pdf

Understanding Needs

Once you have acknowledged a few strengths, you can think about what needs you have. We all have social-emotional needs as well as physical needs. Social-emotional needs include safety and security, a sense of belonging, and a sense of control. Safety and security incudes physical safety as well as a sense of trust in your coworkers and program. Without a feeling of safety, it is hard to be fully present for the children. A sense of belonging comes from having trust in and from your coworkers and the families you serve. In addition, you need to feel appreciated. Educators need to be recognized for what they bring to a classroom. It is a parallel process: if the adults don't feel a sense of belonging, it is difficult or impossible for the children in their class to feel a sense of belonging.

People also need a sense of control. This does not mean you should try to control every aspect of the classroom—that is impossible! But you do need to feel that you have some control. It may seem contradictory, but gaining a sense of control requires you to let go of some control.

Kelley tried to read a book to the children in her family care program. She worried that the children would be disruptive, so she sat an infant on her lap and had the five preschoolers and two toddlers sit in a circle, each on a carpet square. She told the children to sit crisscross applesauce, not touching others, with their eyes looking at the book. When the preschooler Timothy knelt, she stopped reading the book to remind him to sit crisscross applesauce. He sat back down but was soon looking behind him, where he saw a toy on the floor that hadn't been put away. Kelley called, "Timothy, eyes on me." He looked at the book but soon looked back at the toy again. He picked it up and walked over to the basket to put it away. Kelley called out, "Timothy, we need to stay on our carpet square." By this point, the two toddlers had walked away to look at other books on the bookshelf. Kelley was frustrated and said they would finish the book later.

In this example, Kelley is trying to get a sense of control by directing when, where, and how children sit and even where they look. Kelley then spends much of her time directing children rather than reading the book. Soon other children lose interest. Meanwhile, Timothy hears his name called out repeatedly because he is unable to follow all of these directions. I have done the same things at times in my teaching career. When I feel most out of control, I end up demanding more from children. I have found that if I rely on the guideline "we take care of each other" rather than micromanaging children, more children pay attention. Kelley could have sat down with the book and read it to a few interested children while the others played. If Timothy was listening but then moved away to pick up the toy he saw on the floor, she could keep reading. Other children would probably come over. If a child or two got too loud for others to hear the book, she could use the guideline and ask them to either move to another part of the room or be quiet enough so the other children could hear the book. In this sense, Kelley could have felt more in control by being less controlling.

Ask these questions and other similar ones to identify your own social-emotional needs and preferences:

- What actions help build trust with you?
    - others listening to you
    - listening to others
    - consistency
    - mutual sharing of stories
- What actions give you a sense of belonging?
    - clear communication with others at your program
    - social connections with others (small talk)
- What variables can you control in your classroom? What variables are out of your control?
    - Which of these variables tend to trigger you?

www.redleafpress.org
/iiu/qr-1.pdf

- What is grounding for you?

  - What is a grounding activity you can do with children in the classroom?

  - What is a self-care activity you can do in the evening or weekend?

  - Who is someone you can talk to when stressed?

Physical needs for adults generally fall into two categories: accessibility needs and sensory needs. You need all materials and areas of the classroom to be accessible to you. There might be nooks that fit only children, but you need to be able to interact with the child in the nook.

Sensory needs can be more difficult to notice; our senses can *feel* universal because we use them to perceive the world, but they vary from person to person.

Miss Frankie, a preschool teacher, was playing restaurant with a few children. Nearby, Tiffany, a rambunctious four-year-old, was banging a toy school bus on a metal cabinet. Frankie raised her voice and said, "Tiffany, too loud!" Tiffany pushed the bus on the floor. After a minute, she remembered how the cabinet echoed when she banged the bus on it. She started banging the bus on the cabinet again. This time Miss Frankie said, "Tiffany, if you can't use the bus correctly, you will have to find something else to play with."

Miss Frankie was stressed by the loud sound of Tiffany banging the bus on the cabinet so she quickly shut down Tiffany's actions. But Miss Frankie's statement that it was "too loud" is a personal judgment. It may have been too loud for Miss Frankie, but Tiffany was enjoying the sound and it was not too loud for her. This is a case of competing needs.

Miss Frankie gets stressed with sounds at this volume, while Tiffany was listening to the subtle echo that followed the boom of the metal. If Miss Frankie acknowledged her need to not hear that loud sound, she could have problem solved with Tiffany using the conflict resolution model mentioned in chapter two. Each person could have their needs met, and Tiffany would have learned about the different sensory needs people have—perhaps reminding Miss Frankie about these needs as well.

In order to fully support children's diverse sensory diets, you need to understand your own. When you are in the classroom, it is important to recognize what sensory stimuli cause you stress, even if this stress is typically mild, as well as understanding what you can and cannot control. Young children will be loud. If loud noises cause you stress, you can recognize that and plan to take deep breaths or use self-talk to remind yourself that the room is louder because the children are engaged and joyful. It is easy to let our own reactions as the adult in the room dictate what happens, coercing children to assimilate to our needs. Often when children are having fun and getting loud, an adult will "remind" them to "use indoor voices." With self-reflection, you can remember to take deep breaths and then appreciate the play that is happening in front of you. This will decrease your stress while including the children and their play in the classroom. Later in this chapter when you reflect on your classroom, you will see which children are most like you and which are not. You will need to be more intentional with the children who have different sensory diets from yourself. These children may cause you more stress because their sensory diets differ from yours.

Here are some considerations to help you identify your sensory profile:

- I often choose or often avoid activities that are like this:
    - messy/hands-on
    - cerebral
    - loud
    - quiet
    - active
    - calm

www.redleafpress.org
/iiu/qr-2.pdf

- During a typical day, I often do the following:
  - notice a shirt tag or wet sleeve
  - bump into things
  - lean on a wall or table when I am standing

Reflection and Managing Stress

Our work in early learning is stressful, and sensory stimulus is just one of the reasons. Even expected behaviors that are typical for children's ages cause us stress at times. Self-reflection can help us recognize when we are stressed.

Consider how your body holds tension when you are stressed. Is it in your shoulders? Your jaw? Does your heart beat faster? All of these are typical. Learning to recognize when you are feeling this way allows you to respond to your tension. At first, you may notice only after you have raised your voice or made a snap decision, but with self-reflection, you may identify signs that you can pick up on earlier next time. Learning your own signals will help you prevent yourself from reaching dysregulation while improving your relationships with all children. Self-reflection can also help you plan proactive steps to take to minimize stressful situations in your classroom. Engage in whatever play makes you relax every day, drawing, reading, singing, and so on. Don't wait until you find yourself tensing up.

You may find yourself treating some children differently because you get stressed by some of their behaviors. Are you calling out a child's name repeatedly to stop a certain behavior? Are you becoming stubborn, insisting a child do something immediately, such as putting away the blocks they are playing with, without any discussion with the child? Are you talking about this child with coteachers away from the class? Are you avoiding this child, interacting with them less to avoid having to give directives? These are typical reactions, but they are not conducive to building a relationship with that child or supporting them in gaining new relationship skills.

You can also predict common situations that typically cause more stress. For example, on days with inclement weather, I remind myself that the children will probably be louder when they are playing. It may feel like they are "out of control," but the louder voices are a way to work out the everyday stress of being in a group of people, stress that usually is worked out by running and climbing outdoors.

You can address this stress in yourself via strategies to use in the moment and strategies to use when you reflect later. In the moment, you need to address the physical tension in your body and slow yourself down. Here are a few ways:

- Take three deep breaths, and repeat as necessary.

- Take the child's perspective, even moving to their physical level to try to see the situation from their literal point of view.

- Engage in self-talk, reminding yourself that the child is doing the best they can with the tools they have.

- Make a mental note of what skills you may want to foster with this child when neither of you is emotionally heightened.

- If there is a coteacher, swap out with them.

- Redirect children without stopping their play.

- Start an activity that helps you regulate.

Redirection is when an adult guides a child to modify what they are doing. It is not telling a child to do a different activity. If a child is making loud siren sounds while pushing a fire truck, a teacher could command the child not to be so loud. Or the teacher could redirect the child by pointing to a shelf and saying, "Firefighter, my house is on fire. Can you help me?" The child has a choice in the matter. When I am seeking to redirect some behavior, I find it helpful to think about the verb, the action the child is doing. If I notice a child about to throw a block toward a basket a few feet away, I could say, "I'm worried someone could get hurt by the block. What could we throw that wouldn't hurt?" If the child cannot come up with an alternative, I might suggest other items to throw, such as stuffed animals, pillows, or squishy balls.

It is important to know which activities help you regulate in the classroom. For me, these include telling and acting out stories, molding with clay, and reading books. Being aware of my needs helps me stay regulated so I can minimize my own stress.

Using the information from your sensory profile on pages 73–74, which of these common classroom activities help you regulate?

- reading books to the children
- acting out stories
- pretending and role-playing with the children
- dancing to music
- using clay or other heavy materials
- drawing or painting
- building with blocks
- running around with children
- roughhousing with children

www.redleafpress.org
/iiu/qr-2.pdf

In conjunction with using these strategies in the classroom, when you find yourself getting stressed, it is also important to reflect later using the questions below. This allows you to address any stress you may still be carrying, identify proactive strategies to use the next time a similar situation comes up, and plan to foster skills in children that will help them in the future. You can reflect alone or with another person. If you have a coteacher, choose a calm time to discuss together which situations tend to make you more stressed. Your coteacher can potentially step in before you even notice you are getting stressed, and you can do the same for them. It can be much easier for another person to identify when we are getting heightened emotionally.

Ask these reflection questions after a stressful incident:

- How were you feeling at the time?
- Why do you think you were feeling that way?
- How are you feeling now about the situation?
- What other situations cause you stress?

Finally, if you find yourself frequently calling a certain child's name, raising your voice to the child, or avoiding the child, make a point to play with that child more. Building your relationship will most likely decrease the behavior that stresses you. The more you get to know the child, the better you will be able to reflect on the child's strengths and needs. I like to think of it as being on the same team as the child. What is the child's goal? What tools do they currently have? What tools might help?

Danielle, a family care provider, found herself using a tone of voice with three-year-old Calista that showed she was frustrated. When Danielle reflected on this, she realized this usually happened when she was talking to another child and Calista tried to get her attention. Danielle prided herself on really tuning in to the child she was talking to, and Calista's attempts at getting her attention felt like disruptions to Danielle. Danielle realized her need was focusing on the child she was talking to and Calista's need was connection. Danielle reflected on how both needs could be met. The next day, Danielle talked to Calista about their conflicting needs. She asked Calista if Calista would hold her hand while she waited for a turn to talk. Calista agreed.

It can be difficult to admit we are doing something that we know is not best practice, as Danielle did in noticing her tone of voice. If we are going to change our practice, however, we have to take note and reflect on our actions. The point is not beating ourselves up about it but instead making changes. In this case, Danielle noticed she used this tone of voice with Calista at least once a day, which made her reflect on why. She also noticed it happened when she was talking to others. She realized that her needs and the needs of the child she was talking to conflicted with Calista's needs.

For the purposes of reflection, it is not important to distinguish between a preference and a need except to remember that an unmet need may cause a child to dysregulate. A dysregulated child will need to calm down, or regulate, before you can problem solve with them.

Regulation and co-regulation is discussed in chapter five. Even if a child is not dysregulated, I think it helps to acknowledge the child's emotions before problem solving so they feel seen or heard and thus will be more engaged.

Reflection and Cultural Awareness

As mentioned in previous chapters, cultural disconnects may arise when our cultural expectations differ from a child's cultural expectations. If we reflect on our own cultural expectations, including our beliefs, values, and behaviors, we are more likely to recognize cultural disconnects. Our culture affects how we perceive the world, so the world can seem to exist only as we perceive it, making it hard to see our own culture. It is only through exposure to other cultures and self-reflection that we start to see our own culture.

I grew up in a two-parent family, and only my father worked. My mother volunteered at my school and attended every meeting or parent-teacher conference. When I first started teaching, I thought I would simply let parents know when the conferences were, and everyone would sign up. I quickly learned that wasn't the case. My first impulse was to think that these parents were failing their children by not signing up. The director at my center helped me reflect on this feeling. If I were a single parent and relied on child care to go to work, what would I do with my children after child care closed so I could attend the parent-teacher conference? What if I used public transportation and worked two jobs and didn't have time between jobs to get to a parent conference? What if my spouse and I were in the middle of a divorce and we were disputing who went to the conference?

My reflections helped me put things in perspective and then ask parents for alternative ways to share my observations on their child. It's important to note that three decades later, I still feel this same impulse to wonder why parents don't participate. My implicit bias, believing that parents don't show up to school events because they don't care enough, is still with me. Self-reflection allows me to recognize that—make it explicit—and then address this feeling.

Reflecting on your cultural perspective is a lifelong commitment. Your personal cultural perspective is an important part of your identity and a part of what makes you the person you are. Reflecting on your culture isn't an attempt to get rid of your own culture (even if it were possible). The goal is to recognize that your perception is not shared universally. It is easy for us to make assumptions about why others behave the way they do based on our own cultural perspectives. We must always try to understand other perspectives and work toward a common solution rather than assume that others should adapt to us. When reflecting on your cultural perspective, keep in mind the many facets that make up culture, including ethnicity, gender, class, ability, and educational background. While these are not the only facets of culture, these will strongly influence your perspective on your classroom, especially when you do not share the same identity as your coteachers, the children, and their families. Reflect on other, perhaps less obvious, aspects of your culture if they seem to differ from a child or family and create misunderstandings.

When I first started teaching, I had many Anishinaabe students. I remember one day telling children it was time to clean up. Unsurprisingly, most children kept playing. I called across the room to Hinto and Cheyenne, two Anishinaabe children. They stopped playing but just looked down, which made me call out their names again since I wanted eye contact. My assistant teacher, Debbie, who was Dakota, walked over to them and talked to them quietly and they began cleaning up. Debbie later told me that most Native American cultures view direct eye contact as disrespectful, and calling out children's names is shaming. Upon reflection, I realized that I saw eye contact as a way others showed they were listening to me. I have since learned that many cultures generally refrain from eye contact, as do many autistic people. I still make eye contact with others when they talk to me, but if they do not return eye contact, I understand that this is not a sign that they are not engaging with me.

You may self-reflect on your own cultural perspective in reaction to specific situations, but it is also important to reflect more generally on an ongoing basis. One of the best ways to do this is to expose yourself to other cultures. This could be going to events where you are a cultural outsider (assuming outsiders are welcome), watching movies, reading books, listening to podcasts, or traveling to other regions or countries. However, exposing yourself to other cultures is not enough; you must also reflect on your experience and consider the similarities and differences you noticed.

Recognizing other cultural perspectives is different than judging that one cultural practice is better than another. This self-reflection is not an exercise in seeing how wrong your perspective is, nor is it an exercise in thinking other people just need to learn to be like you. Rather it is a way to experience and appreciate the wide range of thoughts and ideas that come from a diversity of cultures.

Finally, self-reflection on your culture includes reflecting on your implicit biases. Implicit bias is the attitudes and/or behaviors you have toward others. By definition, you are probably unaware of them, and they often contradict your stated beliefs, like the example of my reaction to parents not signing up for conferences. Implicit bias develops through repeated experiences in our lives. Our brain processes information by lumping it into categories and making quick decisions based on emotions. This can be positive in some situations, but it can lead to cultural assumptions, including indirect messages that allow us to categorize things in ways that do not line up with our stated beliefs. For example, if a diverse group of candidates is running for president in the United States, the white male candidates may "feel" more "presidential" to many. This is due to the repeated exposure to news images, movies, fiction, and so on that depict presidents as white and male. Someone who has a gut feeling about certain candidates being more presidential than others may *consciously* believe that a Black person or a woman has the same abilities to be president but is more prone to notice indications that a BIPOC or female candidate is lacking in ways that they would forgive in a white male.

There is evidence that implicit bias shows up in classrooms, for example in whose names we call out frequently. This chiding does not have to be harsh for other children to think of these children as the "bad" children. We don't have to use a term like *bad* out loud; children pick up on our patterns, such as repeatedly telling a child to sit down or pay attention. In the United States researchers have found that Black boys are expelled or labeled "special needs" at a much higher rate than others, even though the same behaviors are observed equally in other boys. In addition, behaviors that boys tend to exhibit, such as running inside, are often labeled inappropriate for a classroom. Classrooms could be adapted to allow these behaviors, but instead the children are expected to adapt to the classroom (Gilliam 2005).

Implicit bias is difficult to see in ourselves. The good news is that it gets easier the more you use reflection. But identifying your biases is only the beginning. Addressing them is a lifelong process. If you notice that the behaviors you find most challenging tend to be done by boys, you can look closely at those behaviors and try to understand them. You may find that behaviors you perceive as negative, such as pushing during pretend play, are seen as positive by the children playing the game. Knowing that can change your attitude. In the heat of the moment, however, you still may have the urge to stop that type of play even though you decided months ago that you should allow it. The more you reflect on your own implicit bias, the less likely it is to affect your actions (Brown, Vesley, and Dallman 2016).

It can help to reflect on specific aspects of culture. Next is a list to start you off. You don't need to answer all the questions in one sitting. The list is not exhaustive, and you may add questions that relate to your particular work environment. For example, if you work with military families, what messages did you receive about the military as a child? If your program has many Indigenous families and you are not Indigenous, reflect on messages you received about the specific tribes you work with or Indigenous people in general. Reflect on messages you received as a child about various facets of culture. Here are some examples:

What messages did I receive as a child about the following?

- race
- gender
- disabilities
- children
- elders
- authority
- school
- eye contact

www.redleafpress.org
/iiu/qr-3.pdf

- independence and interdependence
- direct or indirect language
- personal space

Here are a few sample answers of my own:

Race

- Race is not something you talk about. You don't describe the color of a person's skin.
- TV shows and movies will always have people who look like me.

Gender

- Boys are loud and play rough. Girls engage in sit-down activities.

Disabilities

- Disabled people should be pitied. They need our help.

Eye contact

- Making eye contact when someone talks to you shows respect and shows I am listening.

Independence and interdependence

- It is better to do things independently.
- Asking for help is a sign of weakness.

Reflecting with Others

While reflection can be done in isolation, I strongly encourage you to also reflect with others. This is especially important when you are considering your work with children of different cultures and abilities. Having different perspectives when doing this work is vital. This is true even if the people you reflect with share roughly your same race, ethnicity, gender, and abilities because no one shares the same life experiences. Others may have insight from an experience or something they have read. In addition, having an outside eye can help you see a situation differently.

Another way to keep an outside eye on your interactions with children is to use video. Having a second person reviewing a video with you allows you to have a conversation about very specific actions you took. This can be intimidating at first. I find it helpful to think about what I am looking for before I watch a video of myself. For example, I may simply watch to see how often I say children's names to redirect them or otherwise give them commands. This helps me focus on the teaching practice rather than how my voice sounds or how I look in the video. Video can also be used for self-reflection.

When you first start using video, remember you are just trying to capture interactions. I find that I can often just hold my phone in my hand without pointing it at anything or leave it on the table where I am sitting. Most of the time, just hearing voices is enough.

Earlier in my teaching career, I watched a video of myself reading a book to a group of children. It was the first time they had heard the book, and they were excited about what would happen next. I responded to their ideas as they called out. When I watched the video, I could see that I interacted with children to bring out more ideas, building on what they said.

I watched the same video a second time and this time I focused on the children who didn't speak up. Did some of them have ideas that they weren't able to share? Did some of them need a little more time to think about the possibilities before suggesting what might happen? The truth is, I didn't know. All I could see were children watching the book. They did all seem engaged, but I realized I was relying on my own preference for thinking through things verbally. I didn't try to include the voices of the children who were less verbal. Some of them may have preferred to not say anything, but I am sure there were a few who would have spoken up if I had used other strategies.

I made a note next time to pause during a book and ask if anyone else had ideas. I would approach quieter children after I read the book so we could talk one-on-one.

If you work in a center or school, you can reflect with coteachers, other teachers from your center, a director, or educators from other programs. When you reflect with your coteacher, one benefit is that you are both familiar with the children, and it also allows you to help each other stick to any shifts in practice you decide on. Another teacher or a director from your school may have a cursory knowledge of the children you talk about, giving you a combination of insider and outsider perspectives. If you are a family care provider, you can find another provider to be your regular reflection partner.

You can take this one step further and put together a group of a few educators who meet regularly to reflect on your practices. The group can be educators from one center, a few family care providers, educators from several centers or schools, or any combination of these. You can meet in person or virtually. It helps to keep the group small; two to five participants is probably ideal. You can also have a bigger group that breaks up into small groups for discussion. Scheduling a regular meeting every month or every other month should be enough to keep the momentum going but not burn out the participants.

Regardless of how you meet or if you self-reflect alone, the questions should be open-ended and focus around your experience. You can use the questions listed throughout this chapter, take note of other questions as they come up, or share stories. While there may be some venting, it is important to identify what you can learn from the situation, what actions you want to repeat, and what you might want to do differently.

Reflecting on the Classroom Community

In our self-reflection, we often focus on the children who cause us the most stress, but we must make a point to regularly reflect on the whole classroom community, including the adults. Each child and adult in the classroom contributes to the community. Sometimes one individual's interests or personality conflict with another's. It can help to think about how the combination of each person's strengths, needs, and preferences fits together to make a community. In some years, my classroom was fast moving with lots of physical play. Other years, it was full of children drawing and painting with only a handful of children not sitting down.

My role was often helping the children who didn't share these same interests feel included, helping the one child who is making a block building feel that they belong just as much as the six superheroes speeding around them. We as educators set the tone with our beliefs, values, and behaviors. We want to foster diversity, tolerance, and a sense of community.

The next table is a way to roughly identify the members of your class. For each sensory experience, list the names under the headings *avoids*, *neutral*, or *seeks*. List all children and adults in the classroom. There will be more nuance

www.redleafpress.org
/iiu/qr-4.pdf

Sensory Experience	Avoids	Neutral	Seeks
Loud sounds			
Quiet sounds			
Lots of images or bright colors			
Bright lights			
Lots of motion (self or others)			
Messy activities			
Tags or other light touches			
Touching objects with hands			
Tasting unfamiliar foods			
Smelling subtle odors			
Bumping into things			
Wearing or carrying heavy things			
Falling frequently			
Spinning frequently, being off-balance			

than what this table accounts for—for example, some children are stressed by low-pitched sounds but not high-pitched ones. Make adjustments as needed.

With an ongoing reflective practice, you will increasingly notice barriers to child engagement that exist in your classroom. You may even discover how some of your own actions or statements contribute to these barriers. The good news is that your reflective practice will clarify what you can do to be on the same team as each child, sharing the same goal.

Your reflection is only part of the picture, however. You need to rely on multiple experts. This includes the developmental experts that we often think of. It is important to see the child, the family, and their community as experts as well.

Chapter Four

Multiple Experts

The last step in the transition from barriers to bridges is rethinking the idea of who is an expert. The ultimate goal of inclusive child care is that every child and adult feel a sense of belonging in the classroom. A sense of belonging comes from the individual. The educator can make every attempt at including children, but they are successful only if all members of the classroom community feel that sense of belonging for themselves. Therefore, each individual is an expert in creating an inclusive classroom.

This is an inversion of the predominant idea of experts. I think this is partially why so many of us feel unprepared for working with disabled children, since it is often thought of as the realm of special education teachers. This is not to discount the knowledge and expertise of those in special education but rather to lift up those who may not have an academic degree but have learned to become attuned to children of various abilities.

I am not saying that each child is the *only* expert. I believe a constellation view of experts is helpful when working with diverse learners. The child and their family are the primary experts. A strategy, accommodation, or intervention is appropriate only if the child responds favorably and the family allows it. The educator becomes an expert with reflective practice and tuning in to each child. Relevant cultural communities and child development and medical experts also inform the decisions the educator makes.

It should be noted that including multiple experts can lead to multiple ideas. You as the educator must judge what is best for the individual child and the classroom community while they are in your care. Some situations will require more input from a specialist, others from the family or cultural community, and some from observations of the child. Ultimately you have to make decisions for your classroom, just as the parents make decisions for their home, but remain open to feedback from others.

Individual Expert

In previous chapters I talk about being on the same team as the child, sharing a goal. You don't want to be too quick to decide what a child should be doing at any given time. The child will know what they need better than anyone. The child is the embodied expert. In other words, any need, behavior, or ability resides in their body. You can view the child's behavior as communication about their needs beyond what they are able to verbally articulate.

Part of the adult's attunement is gaining an understanding of the child through observation. As mentioned in chapter one, attunement involves observing, reflecting, interacting, then observing again, and continuing the cycle. For example, it happens when an infant cries and the adult guesses what the infant needs. The needs of an infant are mostly focused on the physical and the social: feeding, diaper changing, hugging, and so on. A toddler or preschooler has a wider variety of needs, so the adult has more to consider when trying to understand their behavior. If a child is engaged in activities that interest them, they are most likely doing fine.

As you get to know the child, pay attention to their choices in social interactions. If a child plays alone almost exclusively or watches others play, it may be their preference, but it may also be a lack of skill in interacting with peers. Try partnering in play with the child. Don't force yourself on them, but rather play with the same materials near them in parallel play. If they pay attention to what you're doing, you may slowly enter play with them. Follow the child's cues, and if they respond positively, play with them. While you are with the child, you can describe what other children are doing. You should get a sense if they are interested in joining others at this point. If they are, you can coach them, modeling how to join the others in play.

As mentioned, there is evidence that disabled children have a harder time initiating and maintaining social interactions than nondisabled children (Recchia and Lee 2013). I believe that children don't always know how to attune to others who have different social strategies or skills, but I know that pairing children together or finding roles for disabled children based on their strengths leads to disabled children having more friends. Just as we need to focus on attuning to each child, we can identify when children are not attuning to each other and build bridges between them.

The previous chapter focuses on using reflective practice to understand children's strengths, needs, preferences, and cultural expectations. Now I want to focus on what the child is trying to do, the child's goal. Understanding this goal helps you know what, if anything, you can do to be on the same team. To do this, you need to know what is behind the behavior—or have a good guess. I think there are three basic reasons for a child to exhibit a behavior:

- connecting with others
- attempting to engage or move
- feeling dysregulation and attempting to regulate

Connection is sometimes referred to as "seeking attention." Connecting with others is a basic human need, and children attempt to connect using the skills they have, like the child saying the word "poop" because other children laugh. It's not the only way to make others laugh, but it is a reliable one. Children may also try to connect by getting other reactions from peers, such as pushing or grabbing toys. This is a quick way to connect with others, even if it is short-lived and creates negative feelings in the other child.

When you start to see these interactions as seeking connection, you can talk about it. "You are pushing Khadijah. Did you want to play with her?" If the child says they do want to play with her, you can talk about ways that might be more successful, such as asking her or playing nearby. Foster relationship skills with the child by playing with them and modeling those skills. You can also use storytelling, puppets, and books to start discussions about relationship skills.

I had a child who was curious about whether their toy truck would disappear down the toilet the way their poop did and did not understand that this would clog the toilet. My understanding that cause and effect was an emerging concept for this child and the importance of this child's curiosity helped me appreciate that this incident was not a case of a child being defiant. I understood that the child did not mean to clog the toilet—but I still talked to them about what we put in the toilet. I then thought about what I could control to encourage their curiosity without endangering the plumbing and added funnels and PVC pipes to our sandbox outside so the child could experiment further. In this case it was important for me to understand the child's goal and not focus on my perspective of feeling upset because we needed to fix the toilet.

A child may want to engage with something, but the timing doesn't fit with the adults' agenda. I had child in my class who liked to build but did not like how busy or noisy the block area got. The solution the child came up with was to build while the rest of the class cleaned up. I discussed the issue with the child, and in our conversation we found a simple answer: we added a second place for blocks away from main thoroughfares so the child could build with fewer people around during playtime.

Another type of engagement that comes up frequently is children moving when an adult expects them to sit still. People pay attention by moving to keep the brain alert. Adults often shift in their seat, crossing and uncrossing their legs and arms while sitting and listening. Children's brains have the same need, but they often move their whole body. Children under the age of eight often move for this reason.

Children also move as part of healthy development. Infants are born with reflexive movements. Repeated movement leads to intentional movements as infants become toddlers. Toddlers and preschoolers need lots of physical activity so these movements can become automatic. An automatic movement is one that a person can do while engaged in an unrelated action, such as pouring a cup of water while talking to a teacher. A preschooler will stop pouring to answer a question or the cup will overflow because the child cannot pay attention to both movements simultaneously. Neither movement is automatic but rather requires conscious attention. Automation of movements also allows more precision. Arm and leg movements automate first, allowing the child to focus on fine-motor skills. For example, toddlers paint and draw moving their whole arm. Over time, arm movements become automated, and they focus their attention on wrist and finger movement. Eventually, children move very little at the shoulder and elbow joints when painting or drawing and rely on fine-motor skills. Toddlers and preschoolers need to move for a majority of their awake hours to automate these movements. At first most of this movement will be large-motor—walking, running, rolling, spinning, falling, and so on. If children are allowed to move in these ways, most will gradually lessen these bigger movements and spend more time engaged in fine-motor activities, such as drawing or building with blocks or other toys.

It's less important to understand why young children need to move their bodies but incredibly important to know they *must* do so. Educators should allow for children's movements unless it goes against the guideline "we take care of each other." Is a child pacing while a teacher reads a book "taking care of others"? It's fine as long as the other children can see and hear the book. But if a child is swinging their arms in a way that might hurt someone, that action is not taking care of others. We can expect that some preschoolers will need to move even when listening to a book for the reasons mentioned. If we put ourselves on the same team as these children, we can help them pursue their goal for movement while still allowing all the children to see and hear the book.

Dysregulation is another reason for a behavior. As mentioned earlier, dysregulation can be thought of as when the fight, flight, or freeze response kicks in. It sometime manifests as a "tantrum" or "meltdown"—the point at which a child is not able to talk about what is going on. This is not the time to reason with a child. It is also unhelpful to explain to a child the "consequences" of their actions at this time. They must calm down before you can talk about what harm they may have caused and what they can do to repair it.

You should not threaten any "consequences" for a child's actions, whether it is an attempt to engage with others, an attempt to move, or dysregulation. You are on the same team as the child. You can remove barriers and teach them the skills they need for future situations, but threatening them with consequences puts you in opposition with the child and makes you the "expert" on what should happen. In essence, consequences exclude the child from the process.

Instead, try to learn what caused the behavior. Are they trying to connect with you or another child? Are they trying to move their body? Are they dysregulated because of sensory issues? Are they complaining about it being too loud or too bright? Are they jumping, rocking, pacing, or otherwise repeating movements? Movement is a way to regulate or calm down, and it is a sign that the child is figuring out what they need to do so they can engage with the classroom again.

You can reflect on your observations of the child's behavior using questions similar to those covered in the previous chapter:

- Which of these broad goals most closely fits this behavior?
  - connection with others ("seeking attention")
    - attempts to engage or move (trying to do something at an inconvenient time or place)
    - showing a fight/flight/freeze reaction (something is causing them to dysregulate)
- What is my goal when this behavior is expressed?
- What can I do to be on the same team as the child?
- Are there skills I can nurture with the child?

www.redleafpress.org
/iiu/qr-5.pdf

If the behavior stems from dysregulation, ask these questions:

- Is there sensory stimulus causing them to dysregulate?

- What patterns do I notice when they get dysregulated? (During cleanup time or other "chaotic" times? Wearing certain clothes?)

Answering these or similar questions can help you identify possible changes to make to the environment, skills to model and teach, and conversations to plan with children. This information is important, but you will often need more. Parents and other family members are the next experts to learn from.

Family Experts

In early childhood education programs, we commonly say that parents, guardians, or other primary caregivers are the experts on the child. They are usually the most attuned people to the child in your care. They often don't know the jargon of the field of early childhood education, but they can feel when something is or isn't right for their child. Thus it is important to build bridges with the families as well as the children.

Families have hopes and dreams for their child that should inform your interactions with the child. These hopes and dreams will be embedded in the culture of the family and may be different than what you envision for the children in your care. This is why you should view the parents as experts. It is helpful to give families a chance to express these hopes and dreams. This can be done at a home visit prior to starting in your program or when the family visits your program. You can also make this part of an intake form or a get-to-know-you email— but be sure that the family receives any needed support to fill out forms, especially if there is a language or technology barrier.

During these initial conversations, you can say something along the lines of "I will do my best to meet your child's needs. I know you and your child are experts in those needs, so please let me know if you think there is more I could be doing" (Brown, Vesley, and Dallman 2016). It may be appropriate to acknowledge differences in these conversations. The educator could say, "I haven't worked with a child who uses AFOs (an ankle-foot orthosis or brace). I will read up on the topic while also learning from Haley herself, but I may have questions. I also know that some of what I read may not apply to Haley or your family, so I will make sure to let you know how it's going in the classroom, what is working and what isn't."

Parents' or guardians' ideas of what their child needs may not always be in line with what you observe in a child. For example, families of disabled children often go through a stage of acceptance where they want the child to be treated "the same" as other children. This often happens when the diagnosis is fairly new, so you will probably encounter this attitude if you are working with young children. This focus on equal treatment can result in a child not having a specific need met. It is important to think of yourself as a partner with the families in this situation rather than the expert, even if you have a different idea of what is best for the child. You want to be on the same team as the family. Talking about your shared goal of having the child thrive can help. You can let families know that your classroom talks about differences in many ways. Children who know how to zip coats help the others who do not. When children compare who is the tallest or the fastest, you point out ways that each of them is unique. You mention that not everyone celebrates the same holidays.

Parents may also have different ideas about their child's needs when a child is expressing their gender in a way that makes the parents uncomfortable. You still want to focus on the shared goal of the child thriving. Then ask questions to understand the family's concerns (Pastel et al. 2019). Stay in communication with the family and reflect on what you hear them saying. Keep the focus on the child being healthy and happy. Just as families often want to ignore a child's disability when first getting a diagnosis, families with gender nonconforming children often resist seeing this aspect of the child. Your role is to have a classroom where each person is valued for who they are, a place where everyone belongs. You may have to be the advocate for the child at times but always with the hopes of empowering the family to appreciate all facets of their child.

Meanwhile, it is important for you to learn about the cultures of the families in your classroom so that you can better appreciate and understand the children. Let the families know that the children will be talking about their own cultural identity and hearing about their peers' and teachers' cultural identities as well. You can start by asking the families some questions to get to know their cultural identities.

- What do you celebrate? (holidays, other special events or days)

- How do you celebrate these occasions? (special foods, places, activities)

- What does your family like to do together?

- What terms do you use for family members? (Nana, Grandma, Opa)

- What else would you like me to know about your family or culture?

This information will allow for you to have discussions about the diversity in your classroom. Reassure them that you will let them know where the conversations lead. Ask questions as they come up, whether for individual families or as general questions for all families. It is also important to have conversations about physical similarities and differences such as skin, hair, and eye color, as well as different abilities. See chapter two for a few examples.

Talking to children about diversity is a way for them to celebrate who they are while also celebrating the diversity beyond the classroom. I know it was awkward for me to talk about physical differences with children. If you haven't talked about these things before, it may feel awkward at first, but it gets easier the more you do it.

It's also important to consider the different abilities that family members have. If a family member has a physical disability, ask what they need to participate. An adult may be less likely to visit their child's classroom or show up to a parent-teacher conference if it is difficult to access. Many child care centers are in old buildings that are not completely accessible. Programs based in homes are often even less accessible. A blind friend of mine described an afterschool program where she often had difficulty. Some days when she arrived to pick up her child, she would find the room empty. A staff member from another room told her that the class was in the gym, which was on the other side of the school. She then had to navigate the building, which lacked Braille signage. She was a former early educator herself and could have volunteered at the program, but she never felt truly welcome.

We also need to consider everyone's differences when we communicate with families. At the time of enrollment, let families know all the ways you currently communicate. You should use both verbal and written communication to include families. Ask how they prefer communication and who should be included when sending out communication. Check in with families again after a few weeks to see how things are working and ask if any changes would be helpful. Here are some considerations for communication.

Face-to-face communication

- Don't assume the person picking up or dropping off is the only one who should receive information.

- If there is a language barrier, work with the family:

    - Determine whether there is a staff member who can communicate in the home language.

    - Learn key phrases to use in the home language, including greetings, favorite activities of the child ("he painted," "she built with blocks"), and napping, diapering, and other important information.

    - Determine whether there is a family member who should be contacted for more in-depth communication.

    - If at all possible, use an interpreter.

Written communication

- Send photos as well as text.

- If there is a language barrier, work with the family:

    - Avoid idioms since they are difficult to translate.

    - Translate documents that are sent out routinely.

    - Ask if it is better for you to use a translating app or let them translate.

    - Ask what document form works best for them (Microsoft Word doc, PDF, other).

Nathan was the father of Phil (mentioned in chapter one), a preschooler in one of our inclusive classrooms. Phil was receiving therapy services at our agency, so I often emailed Nathan asking for information. These emails usually had a few items listed. I was often frustrated by his lack of response. But a pattern soon emerged. If I sent a follow-up email with one query, he responded immediately. In one of our meetings discussing Phil's recent ADHD diagnosis, Nathan commented that he also had ADHD. After that meeting I reflected on my emails. I usually started with a sentence or two of pleasantries before asking for information. After the meeting, I moved the pleasantries to the end of the email. I put any queries in the subject line. Suddenly Nathan returned my emails within hours.

It is important to have good communication with families. It helps the family and the child feel a sense of belonging. It is also invaluable when you have a concern you want to bring up. As mentioned in chapter two, you may encounter cultural disconnects between you and a child. If you suspect there is a cultural disconnect, it is helpful to consult with the experts on this—the child's family. For example, if you feel that a child doesn't listen to you, ask yourself:

- What am I doing when I address the child?
- What is the child doing that makes me think they are not listening?
- What do I think should happen? What is my cultural expectation?

Then you can find a time to talk to the parent or family member. The conversation could go something like this, "I noticed that when I try to get your child's attention, your child doesn't look at me. I want to be sure I am not making assumptions based on my own culture. When I was a child and an adult called my name, I would look at them and say, 'Yes?' to show I was listening. What happens in your family?"

Community Experts

You can learn a lot from a parents and family members. They usually know the child better than anyone. They can describe the family and culture the child is part of and clarify experiences that you might not otherwise have context for. But there are times it is valuable to experience cultural communities other than your own to gain new perspectives and learn more about your own cultural perspective. This approach is common with both a cultural competency and a cultural humility framework, but there is a question of balance. You want to learn from community experts to complement what you learn from the family when using a cultural humility lens. In addition, you want to learn in the context of the community whenever possible rather than simply reading about the culture.

I was at my first powwow. I had arrived for the Grand Entry at the time listed on the poster only to find that most of the dancers were still getting ready and the emcee was talking to a few others. No one was in a hurry. I looked around for Sunni, a three-year-old in my class. It was my first year teaching in my new home of Minnesota, on the traditional, ancestral, and contemporary lands of the Dakota and Anishinaabe. Like most new teachers, I was learning as much as I was teaching.

The day was filled with drumming, singing, and dancing. I watched the Jingle Dress Dance, the Men's Grass Dance, the Women's Fancy Shawl Dance, and others. But it was the Tiny Tots Dance where I got to see Sunni in action. I remember the bounce step she showed me in class. I remember her telling me how she and her mom sewed the jingles on the dress. I watched her dance with dozens of other young children, surrounded by her community.

I expected to experience unfamiliar music and dance, but perhaps the most surprising thing for me were the things that were familiar. There were as many Anishinaabe teens wearing T-shirts from heavy metal bands as there were wearing shirts representing Indigenous cultures. When a new drum group started playing, several spectators held up their phones to record. Between dances, many of the spectators and drummers were scrolling through their phones.

I went to the powwow as much for my own entertainment as to learn about Sunni's culture. I did learn about Anishinaabe culture, but I also started an annual tradition of attending powwows in the summer. Like most experiential learning, it was not just a list of facts. I saw Anishinaabe culture as a living, breathing culture. I experienced it in context rather than as an exotic *other* that exists outside of my culture.

At the same time, my own culture as a white man was decentered. I did not always understand what was happening, such as when a dance stopped abruptly. Eventually the emcee announced that an eagle feather had fallen. One aspect of my white privilege is that I rarely experience events that are not created with white people as the intended audience. If another culture is presented, it is done in a way for white people to have context. Simply reading about Anishinaabe culture would have given me some information but would probably have explained how it differs from "mainstream"—that is, white middle-class—culture in a binary way.

I started teaching in a classroom that was about one-third Native American, mostly Anishinaabe; one-third African American; and one-third first-generation West African, mostly from Ghana and Nigeria. No one was white like me. Luckily, I was so new to teaching that I didn't pretend to be the only expert. I asked questions when I needed to, but mostly I observed.

I have only recently come to think of my experiences at powwows, Juneteenth celebrations, family barbecues, and other events as learning from community experts. Part of the reason is that being part of these events did not involve explicitly gathering information about a particular culture. In fact, my biggest takeaway was probably the experience of being an outsider and not always knowing what was expected. I had to learn to be humble and learn from those around me and to acknowledge how my experiences have been different. I could ask questions to gain understanding if I did so in a respectful manner. Yet I have to be careful to not think that these few experiences make me an expert in another culture. My experiences give me a better understanding of the context the children are growing up in. Viewing community members as experts acknowledges that my cultural beliefs, values, and behaviors are not the measure of all other cultures.

In my story of going to the powwow, I learned about my own sense of time and how much I am tied to my clock. I also become more empathetic for someone with a different cultural practice. I may have already known that an Anishinaabe parent might not show up for a conference right at 5:30, but now I know they might have stopped at the grocery store on the way and took the time to help an elder carry groceries to their car before heading to the conference. Learning about cultural differences does not mean I view one culture as better than the other. It simply means I can recognize those differences. I find it makes it easier to recognize cultural disconnects when they happen. Getting to know more about a culture also informs your conversations with parents and other family members.

Learning from community experts doesn't have to mean going to cultural events. You can read books, listen to podcasts, and watch videos or movies. Some of your reading or watching may specifically cover parenting or education, but make this one part of a broader cultural understanding. The work does not have to address race or culture explicitly, but it should be created by a member of the community you are reading about. If you are reading a book about a Black family, make sure it is written by a Black author. At the same time, remember that no one individual can speak for an entire community. Somewhat paradoxically, you don't want to rely on one person as the expert on a community; rather, each member of a community will know more than you do about the community.

Community experts can inform educators by helping them see the child and family in a new light and serving as a source of information when the family does not share an identity with their child, such as a disability or race or ethnicity, as in a transracial adoption.

The parents of children with physical or mental disabilities often do not have similar impairments. In some cases, the family can struggle with viewing a diagnosis as anything but a disability, especially when first learning of the condition. As the parent of an autistic child, I know I thought about what barriers my child might face rather than reflecting on my child's strengths and abilities. All parents and guardians go through their own process. Because the children we work with are young, the chances are that the parents are still early on this journey.

Ableism is the discrimination of disabled people, or as Greg Smith, creator of the radio show *On a Roll*, described it, "the devaluation and disregard for people with disabilities" (Smith 2001, 162). Ableism is pervasive in the education and medical fields. The mere idea of inclusive classrooms is only a few decades old, after a hard-fought battle from disability rights advocates. This is why lip reading was used in schools for decades instead of sign language and much of autism treatment has focused on learning to refrain from behaviors that made non-autistic people uncomfortable. The voices of disabled people were ignored.

I have done my best to listen to disability advocates in the writing of this book, but the truth is that most academic writing about disability and education is created by nondisabled people. I hope that this changes. The field of disability studies is growing, but it has made only a slight impact in the field of early childhood education. I think it is up to all of us to listen to the voices of disabled adults. What are the barriers in classrooms today that exclude autistic children? Blind children? Children with oppositional defiant disorder?

In the meantime, I think each of us can become attuned to the children in our care, talk to the families, learn from the communities—especially adults with the same disability as a child in our classroom—and consult with medical or therapeutic experts. Then we need to use our best judgment.

Child Development and Medical Experts

I do not want to give the impression that I think medical experts are not needed. They most certainly are. Medical experts include doctors, therapists, mental health professionals, and other people who focus on the impairment. You as the educator are focused on the classroom community and removing barriers that prevent individuals from engaging in the community. The roles are different.

A medical expert may inform an educator. For example, a therapist might help an educator understand a child's sensory profile and what sights or sounds may be stressful. The information might focus on a particular piece of medical equipment that will be in the classroom, such as an oxygen tank with a tube that follows the child around as they play.

Child development experts research and write about specific disabilities. This information gives us insight into what we might expect for a child with a specific disability, what is typical development as well as what is less typical but still common. I do not want to downplay the importance of this information, but I do also want to offer some caution. While there is some shift, most of the research on child development continues to be done with limited cultural representation, focusing on white, middle-class families with parents who tend to be more educated than average. In addition, most of this research is done in the United States or Western Europe. That is not to say that the information is useless but instead to acknowledge that it might not be the full picture. The current understanding of child development should inform our work as educators, but we should also believe our own eyes if we experience something different. When looking for effective strategies for children of diverse cultures in group settings, I hope more researchers will learn from the many BIPOC family child care providers who provide culturally sensitive care every day. We could be learning from disabled adults about what they think is important for children with the same disability. Adhering to the binary of the "researcher" and the "researched" has limited the knowledge of our field.

Another shortcoming is that most of the research is done outside of a typical group setting (such as family child care, center-based care, or the neighborhood playground), focusing on individual child development as if children do not typically spend much of their time in groups. Moreover, in my experience, I've seen that a child's sensory integration, movement needs, and executive function skills lead to most classroom challenges for educators but are a low priority for research. This is especially evident in most early education programs in higher education, which typically give only a cursory acknowledgment of sensory development and integration. Terms such as *proprioception, interception,* and *vestibular* are often saved for special education or therapy programs even though these concepts are as crucial as *cognitive development*, a term that is often used in general education courses.

You should listen to experts, whether speaking directly to a child's therapist or reading a book on a specific disability, but you should never lose sight of the child or family as you do this. Even when a practice is recommended, you still need to judge whether it is appropriate for a specific child. You are the gatekeeper in your classroom and the expert on your classroom community.

Educator Expert

As the gatekeeper, you decide what makes sense for each child in your classroom and what happens there. Attunement to each child is necessary for you to make thoughtful decisions. All the sources mentioned in this chapter—the child, family, and community, as well as the medical experts—will help you choose what you do in the classroom, but the choice is yours. Remember that the goal is not for the child to assimilate to the culture of the classroom but rather to have the child engage with materials as well as with peers and adults. If the child is not engaging, you can decide if they need more time or if a new strategy is called for. You do not need to always get things right—and indeed, you cannot and will not. What makes you an expert is knowing when something isn't working for everyone, even if it is only one person in your classroom.

When I am thinking of new strategies, I often turn to my reflective practice partners referred to in chapter three. Sometimes I just need to talk through the situation and I think of next steps without much input from my partners. Other times, outsiders' eyes give me new ways to look at the situation or strategy. Sometimes they suggest helpful books or websites. If you do not have a reflective practice partner yet, try reaching out to other educators, whether in your workplace or in your wider community or through social media.

When you are unsure of your next steps, turn back to the children in your classroom and ask them for ideas. If you think one or more of the children could be embarrassed if you bring up a specific situation, you can tell a fictionalized story or use puppets and change a few details.

Once I had a child named Edie who frequently took toys out of other children's hands. At circle time, I used two puppets to act out a scenario in which a cat kept taking a dog's ball. When the puppets asked for ideas from the children, the first child to speak up was Edie. She suggested that maybe the cat really wanted the ball and got so excited they forgot to ask. I then asked Edie what the dog should do. She suggested that the dog could just remind the cat. I acted out the scenario as the child suggested and then said, "Maybe we could try that in our own classroom." Of course, behaviors don't change overnight, but when I heard someone yell at Edie, I approached and calmly said, "Edie, don't forget to ask if you want something." Edie would calm down and ask the other child. Often, the other child would either give the toy to Edie or suggest they play together. It didn't always solve the problem, but the situation happened less frequently.

You are not alone when you are looking for ideas. Part of being an intentional educator is seeking other educators with similar values. Who can you talk to when you are looking for ideas or when you need to calm down after a stressful interaction? Never think that you have everything figured out. The needs of the children and coteachers, as well as your own needs, are always changing. What may have worked for you for the past five years might not work tomorrow. Focus on attuning to children and notice what engages them. Continue to observe children, have conversations with families, learn from communities you don't belong to, and read books and articles. All of this will influence you, but ultimately what you offer children is your authentic self. You model lifelong learning for the children.

I have covered a lot of ground in this book trying to reframe how we view inclusive early learning programs. My hope is that you will feel more confident working with children with different cultures and abilities by focusing on removing barriers and building bridges. I hope that even in the most stressful time, you can remind yourself, "bridges, not barriers." Of course, you need more than a three-word mantra to include all the children in your classroom. The next chapter introduces steps you can take so that every child and adult feels they belong in your classroom.

Chapter Five

Putting It Together

I have framed inclusion as removing barriers and building bridges. This requires a lens of cultural humility where you see yourself as a member of the classroom community with your own cultural perspective. I have asked you to use constellation thinking when you consider the array of strengths, preferences, and needs that you and every person in the classroom have. Reflective practice will allow you to identify the barriers to engagement that children (or adults) encounter and to form strategies to build bridges to include everyone in the classroom. With all this information it can be hard to see what steps to take and when.

In this chapter, I lay out a step-by-step approach to using the ideas from this book. It is important to note that this is not a prescriptive guide with materials and lesson plans but rather a guide for where to focus your reflective practice. I have laid it out into three broad categories: proactive, global, and individual strategies. Proactive strategies focus on how you set up your environment and the relationships you establish with the children and families as they enter your classroom. Global strategies refer to the approach you take with all the members of the classroom, children and adults. These strategies do not expect each person to have the same needs or to behave the same way, but they aim to be inclusive. A few children will struggle despite your best efforts to include them. These children may need individual strategies to help them engage with materials and others.

After you have tried all these steps, a few children may still need additional support. This could be occupational or mental health therapy for a child or a special education coach for the educator. In most cases, the child will still be in your classroom while they receive these other services, but there will occasionally be a child who needs support beyond what you can do. It's important not to take this personally and think of this as a failure on your part. Though I believe we are referring too many children to special education based on a belief that children must assimilate to a standardized classroom culture, that does not mean that there aren't children who truly need specialized services. I believe we all have a responsibility to include children with their unique strengths, preferences, needs, and culture. I have found that these steps have allowed me to do this.

Proactive Strategies

Engagement is the goal for all children and adults in a classroom, so the first thing you must do is remove any potential barriers. It's easiest to start with physical barriers. Design your learning environment with the children and adults you have now. If you have a child or adult (including a parent who might visit) who uses a wheelchair, it is important to be wheelchair accessible, but it is also important to remember that many children like small, cozy spaces. You still want to have these spaces, but make sure that at least part of the cozy space can accommodate a wheelchair. You may also have to adapt the classroom for other visitors.

The class was excited. Our Grand Friends were coming! We usually visit them every Friday morning at the nursing home in the neighborhood. This time, we had arranged transportation for them to see our classroom. At our morning meeting that day, I asked the children how many of our Grand Friends used wheelchairs. They figured out that at least four used wheelchairs, five if Louisa came. Then I asked them if all the wheelchairs would fit in our room. The answer was obvious. I asked the children what we could do. We spent the next twenty minutes rearranging furniture so we were ready to welcome all our Grand Friends. The Grand Friends felt welcome, and the children learned another lesson in diversity.

In addition to physical mobility, it is also important to accommodate the different movement needs of children. Young children need to be moving most of the time as part of their development. Some children need more movement than others. Children need a place to move that they can use throughout the day, in a place where they won't disrupt other types of play. Ideally there should be a designated space with mats. The fact that a designated space for movement is not considered standard practice in early learning settings is an indication of how these practices reflect the culture of the educators and not the needs of the children. If you do not have a designated space, figure out where children can be physically active in your space. Perhaps there is a couch or a corner with pillows. In either case, you should assume that children need to move and plan accordingly.

Some of the movement children need is what occupational therapists refer to as **heavy work**. Heavy work is an activity that pushes or pulls against the body, activating the proprioceptive sense. These types of activities help keep children and adults regulated. Heavy work can happen inside and outside, in play and during classroom tasks.

Climbing, digging, pushing on swings, and roughhousing are examples of heavy work that often happens outside. Building with large blocks, sculpting with clay or playdough, and blowing bubbles are heavy work activities that might happen indoors. Classroom tasks such as sweeping, stacking chairs, and moving cots or other furniture are also opportunities for heavy work.

Finally, when thinking about physical barriers, remember that each child and adult has an individual sensory profile. While you cannot anticipate every sensory need, you should try to allow for a variety of sensory experiences. Having multiple sources of light allows you to adjust the brightness as needed. It is also helpful to have spaces where direct light is blocked, in a cozy corner, under a table, or behind a living room chair. These spaces can also provide a place to get away from louder sounds. Consider how to allot space for messy activities for the children who need a lot of tactile input. If you are prepared to clean up spills and mess, you are more likely to allow them. I always had a pile of old towels on hand for cleanup. Just as you want to have heavy work, plan on having some tactile activity available every day, whether it's playdough, clay, soapy water, paint, or what have you. You will find that some children are calmer during the day if they can squish slime for a few minutes every hour or two. Be sure to plan for activities that help you regulate, too, as discussed in chapter three.

Informational barriers can also be addressed proactively. Children need to understand the who, what, where, when, and why of your classroom. You can create visuals and social stories to help them with this.

Who

- Create a visual of all the children and adults in the class, along with their names.
  - Post it on the wall.
  - Put it into a photo album (or photos on a metal ring) in the classroom.
  - Email it to families.

What

- Post a daily message board that highlights any important information children and adults need to know about the day.

- Use visuals/steps for tasks such as using the bathroom and washing hands.

- Create social stories (*see sidebar*).

  - Make a homemade book that talks through typical scenarios, such as what to do when you are mad and what to expect at school.

Social Stories

Social stories help a child understand what to expect, especially when there are strong emotions involved. A social story gives a child predictable guidance or choices when they are upset. It also allows you, the educator, to be a neutral party simply reading the story. A child who is already upset may accept the advice in a story even if they would react angrily if an adult asked the same questions or gave the same advice directly to the child. Social stories can be written about what to do when you are mad or when you miss your parent. Children may feel less anxiety around starting at child care if they have a story that reminds them of what they can expect to happen or what options they have in a situation. You can find examples of social stories online.

Where

- Label materials.

  - Put a label on the container and the shelf where the container goes.

  - Label them in a way the children can understand (photos, drawings, raised drawings, example of the item, and so on).

When

- Post a visual schedule with pictures for each part of the day.

- Create first/then cards to show common sequences (*see sidebar page 110*).

Why

- Post guidelines focused on what is allowed rather than what is not (*see sidebar page 111*).

First/Then Cards

Make first/then cards using small cards (such as index cards). Draw two boxes, one labeled "First" and the other labeled "Then." In each box, make a simple drawing to represent two actions. It can be as simple as "First school/Then home," or explain a specific routine such as "First wash hands/Then eat." The cards can help when a child struggles with something routine, helping the child picture what happens next. Keep in mind that you want to avoid forcing a child into a routine simply because it is "what we do in the classroom." It should serve the needs of the community, not force the child to assimilate.

Many of these proactive strategies can be revisited throughout the year. You may find you need to rearrange the room because children need more space to move or you uncover unanticipated sensory needs. You may need to add social stories as situations come up.

Here is a checklist of Proactive Strategies:

- To address physical barriers, incorporate:
  - physical accessibility
  - areas for movement
  - allowances for diverse sensory profiles (including your own)
  - heavy work
- To address informational barriers, incorporate:
  - visuals, including members of the class
  - a visual schedule
  - a message board
  - first/then cards
  - posted guidelines

Global Strategies

You use global strategies with all the members of the classroom, children and adults. I find that when an educator is consistently challenged by a child's behavior, they come to me as the curriculum coach to ask for a targeted strategy that will stop the behavior. This is a natural reaction since the educator is emotionally triggered. There are strategies

Guidelines

Guidelines are positive statements that say what children do to keep themselves and others safe, whereas rules state what children cannot do. Guidelines are essentially variations on the golden rule. In my classrooms I use the guideline, "We take care of each other."

to use in the moment when a child is dysregulated, but then it is important to step back and reflect on the global strategies you're using. What are you doing for the whole class? When an educator tries to use individual strategies for each child in the classroom, it gets overwhelming.

Global strategies include having a consistent yet flexible daily schedule, using the guideline "we take care of each other," helping children identify and express emotions, fostering relationship skills, and bringing awareness to diversity. First, create a predictable flow (or schedule) to your day so children know what to expect. It should be consistent and unhurried but flexible. The sequence of events should stay the same as much as possible, but the timing of activities should flow with children's interests. Have as few transitions as possible. Keep the pace unhurried.

You can encourage movement and not just allow it by keeping chairs stacked along a wall instead of tucked under tables. Children can carry a chair over if they would like one, which gives them some heavy work. Heavy work helps bring children's arousal state down if they are stressed from other sensory input, such as the volume of the room or the number of conversations around them. At the same time, children are more likely to incorporate movement even while working at a table if they are standing or kneeling. I have found that this small change resulted in the children who are in constant motion drawing more and the children who draw for hours moving more.

The guideline "we take care of each other" encourages children to assist others if they are unable to do something by themselves. For example, if you do keep your chairs stacked and a child is unable to carry a chair over themselves, another child can bring it over. A few children may be able to zip coats. Others may be able to cut tape or yarn for someone who lacks the coordination. You can encourage the child who needs assistance to ask for help by asking if they know which peers have the skill, or if you sense the child wouldn't know, you can say,

"I've seen Maddie cut yarn. Should we ask her? [Child nods.] Maddie, Eric would like some yarn. Could you cut it for him?" In this way you model how to ask for help. You can also coach the children who have a skill. When children are putting on jackets, you can ask, "If you know how to zip, could you ask others if they want help?" You are teaching them not only to take care of others but to respect them by asking if they want help first. You can thank them afterward. "Thank you for taking care of each other."

One classroom I was coaching had an autistic child named Taji who liked to be greeted by name before he walked into the classroom. He would stand at the threshold until the teachers, Colleen and Anna, greeted him. After this happened a few times, Colleen and Anna made a point of greeting Taji as soon as he arrived. Anna noticed a few children watching with interest. She told them that Taji liked to be greeted and hear his name before he came in the classroom. After that, every child would stop what they were doing and say, "Good morning, Taji," when he arrived.

In this example, Colleen and Anna were showing the children specific ways to take care of one of their classmates. Coaching children to care for others creates bridges between them and makes them more empathetic. Taji sometimes pushed over other children's block buildings. The other children knew that Taji didn't do this out of aggression. If they saw him approaching their buildings, they would remind him not to push it. This didn't happen overnight. Anna helped the children work through anger and explained that Taji was interested in the sound the blocks made, but he wasn't trying to make others mad. Teaching empathy and caring does take time, but it is hard to think of any other learning that is more valuable.

Of course, guidelines also keep children safe in the classroom. If I notice a child is about to throw a block, I can say, "Remember, we take care of each other in our classroom. I'm worried that if you throw a block, it could hurt someone. Is there something you could throw that wouldn't hurt if you accidentally hit someone?" I taught one child who liked to throw small rubber figurines into a basket. He did occasionally hit someone, but the toys were fairly soft, and he would simply apologize and get the toy. Eventually I added rolled-up socks and tiny pillows for him.

Having guidelines doesn't just keep the room safe but also encourages children and adults to problem solve. Each case doesn't have just one solution, and the answer will vary depending on the individual's strengths, preferences, and needs. Problem solving in this way allows the child to feel in control and fosters their self-control.

Another key global strategy is teaching about emotions. Some of this will be "on the fly" as situations happen. But it is also important to give children opportunities to think about these skills when they are not in a heightened emotional state. Reading books about emotions and friendships is a good starting point, but be sure to include discussion questions, such as "How do you think they feel in this picture?" "What could the characters do differently?" and "Have you ever felt this way?" You can tell stories or use puppets and have the children decide how the story gets resolved.

You can also teach children ways to handle their emotions appropriately by supporting them when they are in a heightened state. Young children are still developing the ability to recover from sensory input, cultural disconnect, or strong emotions from a conflict with another child or adult. While it is important to figure out the reason eventually, when a child is upset you must first address the emotion. I find the neurosequential strategy developed by Dr. Bruce Perry to be helpful. The neurosequential approach is simple enough for most adults to use without specialized training. It has three steps: regulate, relate, reason (2020). A child must be regulated before relating to other peers or adults. A child must have a connection to an adult or other child before they can reason. Reasoning for preschoolers can be thought of as engaging in tasks, problem solving, or any other action that requires intentional thought.

Regulate

Regulation refers to having the appropriate arousal level to meet current demands (Chaves and Taylor 2021). If Carmen gives a marker to Janina, Janina will probably smile, take the marker, and possibly say thank you. If instead Janina yelled at Carmen to leave her alone and ran away, that would be a high arousal level. On the other hand, if Carmen pushed Janina, yelling and running away would be an appropriate arousal level (even though we may prefer that Janina tells Carmen to stop). Thus, what is considered regulation can depend on context. The arousal level needed at rest time is different than what is needed when a child is playing pretend with others. Some of this context is imposed by adults. If a child feels the need to move and the adult wants everyone to sit still and listen to a book, there is a discrepancy between the child's arousal level and what the teacher would like. This is a case where the adult could allow for a wider range of arousal levels, such as pacing behind other children, or offer an alternative activity for those who cannot or do not want to sit. With these shifts, the child would be considered regulated for the situation.

When children are not regulated for the situation, occupational therapist Megan Applewick urges us to think of dysregulation as children working to calm their body to a neutral state so they can interact and engage with others (2021). The response may be ineffective, but we should recognize the child's goal. The child does not need an adult to remind them of manners or rules; they need an adult to co-regulate with them. Applewick describes co-regulation as the nurturing adult being in a shared space and relationship with the dysregulated child, working toward soothing and regulating their physical and emotional state. The adult gets down to the child's level and offers physical reassurance, whether that is sitting close, hugging, holding the child on the adult's lap, or sitting a few feet away from the child. While managing their own emotions and arousal levels, the adult can attune and adjust their approach to meet the child's needs (see below for a few ideas). The adult cannot "force" the child to regulate; rather, through relationship and graded supports the child progresses alongside their caregiver back to a regulated state.

The child will eventually meet the adult's arousal state, so it is important for the adult to be calm. Only a regulated adult can help a child regulate. This can be difficult, as a crying, screaming, or hitting child will cause us to be stressed. It is important to recognize your own stress in the moment and breathe deeply. This is where the phrase "bridges, not barriers" may help. Repeat the phrase to remind yourself to calm down. I usually label a child's emotion when I first approach, but then I try not to say anything else until I feel I am regulated enough myself that my tone of voice will be calming.

When you are somewhat calm, you can remind a child to breathe deep. Blowing bubbles or pretending to blow candles or a balloon sometimes helps, as does hugging a stuffed animal, blanket, or pillow. Hugging a trusted adult or peer can help if the child accepts the hug. Even if a child usually accepts a hug, there may be times they do not want one. Swinging and other rocking motions or slow movements are calming for most children. A glitter jar, sensory bottle, or fish tank can all be used. If you are outside or at a window, you can watch birds, cars, or clouds moving in the distance. Chewing on a chew toy or gum provides proprioceptive input, which has a calming effect. Finally, if you think sensory input is contributing to the child's dysregulation, you can help the child move away or remove the source. This could be making the lights dimmer or turning them off or shutting off a fan. You could have the child go under a table or in a tent to calm down.

To sum up, here are the steps to use when trying to help a child when they are dysregulated:

1. Approach calmly.

2. Label their emotions: both the feeling and how it shows up in the body.

3. Assist the child with coping skills:

   ○ taking deep breaths (have the child blow at a pinwheel or blow bubbles)

   ○ hugging a stuffed animal or trusted adult

   ○ swinging or rocking

   ○ watching objects with slow movements (glitter jar, fish tank)

- chewing something appropriate
- moving away from the stimulus that is causing distress

4. Shift your volume or tone if child is not responsive.

Relate

Once a child is regulated or calmed, they can interact with others. The child is unlikely to engage in activities that require higher-level thinking, but social engagement is possible at this point. Now the role of the adult is to continue to be a predictable presence. Having an established relationship with the child is essential. You can offer to do an activity with the child that emphasizes this relationship, such as reading a book together. The child may prefer to be alone or play with peers. Whatever makes them feel part of the classroom community is fine.

Reason

When a child is regulated and feels a sense of belonging, they can use higher-level thinking or reason. In young children, reason shows up as play, exploring materials, negotiating with others, problem solving when something isn't turning out the way a child hoped, and so on. I have found that I often have a desire to jump to problem solving when children are upset, but the neurosequential model reminds me to make sure children are regulated first. It also reminds me that sensory stimuli or social stress can be a barrier for children to engage in my classroom. Just as I would address a physical barrier for a wheelchair user, I need to address situations that consistently dysregulate a child (or adult).

This sequence of regulate-relate-reason also highlights why we need to build emotional, relational, and physical skills in children as part of our global strategies. If we wait until a child encounters an issue that dysregulates them, it is no longer possible to help them with new skills. You can only help them use the skills they currently have.

Some children become dysregulated more than others. If a child becomes dysregulated often and the frequency or duration do not seem to be decreasing, you need to identify individual strategies to support the child.

Along with learning about emotions, children need to develop relationship skills. These skills are often learned in the moment in the same way emotions are, but the educator's attitude is important. First and foremost, you must form an authentic relationship with each child. Think of care tasks such as feeding and dressing children as opportunities for building trust rather than simply a chore. Be curious about each child's interests and personality. Find times to have casual conversations and times to play with each child. Notice the children when things are going well rather than mostly talking to children when you want to redirect behavior. Make occasional comments about what you observe—you don't need to make a running commentary of everything that is happening in the classroom. Take time to appreciate what you see children doing and then acknowledge what you see. "You are really working carefully to make that building so tall." If you notice a child watching others, sit near them and watch with them. After watching for a while, comment on what you see, using the names of the children. "Claire is standing on her toes to get the block on top of her building." This can help bridge the gap if the child who is watching wants to join the play at some point.

Playing with children also builds relationship skills. It is important that the adult join play only when children invite them and that the adult lets the child lead the play. If it is pretend play, have the children choose a role for the adult. Start playing in parallel for most other types of play, using the same materials in roughly the same way. If a child is drawing with markers, don't sit next to them and draw a masterpiece. This discourages many children from drawing, and they will ask you to draw pictures for them instead of with them. Rather, echo the types of marks they are making. I like to play near a child and then wait until they talk to me. Sometimes they suggest we collaborate. Other times they make comments about the play or creation. For nonspeaking children, you can speak first but watch for nonverbal cues to see if they are engaged in the interaction or if they are trying to focus on their solitary play.

When children struggle with relationships skills, whether a child is unsure how to join others in play or a conflict is erupting, you can acknowledge any strong emotions that might be present. "You seem frustrated that she said she didn't want help with her block building." Then you can give a quick suggestion. "Maybe you could make your own building nearby. Then you might be able to have your dinosaurs visit each other's buildings." You might offer to help them get started with their own building. Children are more likely to invite others into their play when they see them playing in a similar way because they aren't fully able to picture what collaborative play would look like. You are acting more as a coach, fostering relationship skills between children while staying on the sidelines as much as possible.

Teaching about relationships also requires you to teach about diversity of identities. Young children begin to notice differences in race, gender, and ability during infancy (Pastel et al. 2019). You can help children learn to talk about these differences in a matter-of-fact way. Reading books is a good way to start these conversations. I learned as a child to avoid these topics, and it can still make me uncomfortable. However, it has gotten easier the more I do it, and I can see how it has a positive influence on children. I have found that acknowledging differences allows the children and adults to appreciate both differences and similarities. Pretending to not notice that a child uses a wheelchair means you are not noticing that child, whereas acknowledging the wheelchair but not making assumptions about what the child can and cannot do honors the child.

In one classroom, four-year-old Linda used a wheelchair. Her classroom was on the second floor and there was an elevator. Her teachers, Kimberly and Paige, thought it was important that Linda was always included. Linda was in Paige's primary care group. Kimberly would lead her group down the stairs to the playground while Paige's group used the elevator because "not everyone in the group can use stairs."

In the spring, firefighters brought a fire truck to the school for the children to see. Paige lifted Linda out of the wheelchair to explore the interior of the fire truck. When Linda was done, the other children were already standing next to the truck for a group photo. Paige lifted Linda out of the truck and turned so they could be in the photo. Linda said she wanted to be set down. As Linda sat on the ground, all the children wordlessly sat down with her. The children were attuned to Linda. They sat down because "not everyone in their class can stand." This did not happen by accident but rather through intentional teaching from Paige and Kimberly.

Before we go into individual strategies, here is a checklist of global strategies:

- Follow a consistent yet flexible daily schedule.
- Refer to your class guidelines:
  - Encourage children to assist peers.
  - Encourage children to appreciate differences.
  - Encourage children to problem solve.
- Teach about emotions.
  - Regulate, relate, and reason.
    - Approach calmly.
    - Label their emotions: both the feeling and how it shows up in the body.
  - Assist children with coping skills.
- Teach about relationships.
  - Form authentic relationships with the children.
  - Use the children's names so they learn the names of their peers.
- Teach about diversity.

Individual Strategies

When children struggle to stay regulated even with global strategies in place, you can try using individual strategies. This requires that you reflect on the child and the situations that seem to cause stress. Some children may cause others stress even if they don't appear to get dysregulated themselves. This can be due to a difference in relationship skills or cultural disconnects. You can also use the same reflection process for these situations.

Here are some reflection questions you can use:

www.redleafpress.org
/iiu/qr-6.pdf

- What behaviors cause distress or disruption?

- How often do these behaviors happen?

- When and where does this typically happen?

- If it's a particular time of the day, what is your goal during this time? (For example, rest time needs to be quiet for those who nap.)

  - What is the child trying to do during this time (connect or engage, or exhibiting dysregulation)?

  - Is there a sensory component to address?

  - Are there emotional or relationship skills that would help?

- Is there a way to be on the same team as the child and share the same goal?

- What are five strengths and preferences of this child?

- Is there a possible cultural disconnect? What might the child's cultural perspective be?

- How can I use these strengths and cultural perspectives to support the child so we can be on the same team?

- What strategies can I try?

Once you have reflected and identified a new strategy, try using it for several days. If the frequency or duration of the behavior decreases, continue the strategy. If it does not seem to have an effect or makes things more stressful, try reflecting again to identify another strategy. If this second strategy is also ineffective, arrange a time to meet with the parents for a partnering conversation.

A partnering conversation is an attempt to build a bridge with the family to understand the child better as well as to share information with the family. You should already have a warm relationship with the family when you arrange this conversation. Ideally you would meet without the child present so you can talk about the child. If the child must come along, remember to acknowledge and address the child rather than talk about them as if they are not there. Emphasize that you want to all be on the same team as the child. Start with the strengths you have noticed in the child. Ask the family to list additional strengths.

Then you can bring up the situation or behavior that causes you concern. Use phrases such as "I have noticed that when we are laying quietly for rest time, Lucinda walks around the room and talks to the other children, some of whom are trying to sleep. I have tried using a visual that shows her that first I will rub backs for those who are going to sleep and then I can talk to her. I have also tried giving her photos of you and the rest of the family while I am rubbing backs, but so far she still walks around talking to others. I know you don't have rest time like we do in the classroom, but I was wondering if you had any ideas? What happens when her baby brother takes a nap?"

Depending on the situation, this would be a good time to find out more about possible cultural disconnects. You can bring this up by talking about your own experience, "When I was growing up, if an adult called our name, we were expected to walk over to them. I know that isn't everyone's experience. In your family, what is expected when a child's name is called?"

At the end of the discussion, identify at least one new strategy to try. Give the new strategy a week or two to take effect. If there is still no change in the frequency or duration of dysregulation or the concerning behavior, you may need to talk to the parent about additional supports.

Partnering Conversation

Some of the child's strengths:

1.

2.

3.

4.

5.

www.redleafpress.org
/iiu/qr-7.pdf

Are there any strengths you (the parent) want to highlight?

Strategies identified to help child succeed:

Observations of the child in the classroom:

What have you experienced?

What new strategy could be used in the classroom?

Additional Supports

If a child is still struggling after you have used the proactive, global, and individual strategies, they probably need additional supports, which can vary. It could include an outside therapist, such as an occupational therapist, a speech-language pathologist, or a mental health provider. Some areas have a special education program available through the public schools—ideally an inclusion program with a specialist on staff who will help with additional individual strategies as the child remains in your classroom. Continue to use global strategies as well as any helpful individual strategies. Whatever the specifics, continue to nurture your relationship with the child. The closer your relationship, the more likely the child will struggle less. I find that teachers can unwittingly pull away from children when they receive other services, perhaps thinking that someone else is helping the child now. Continue to interact with the child and be intentional about connecting with them. Continue to be a bridge and not a barrier.

Here is a checklist of individual strategies:

- Reflect on the child's strengths as well as the concerning behavior or situation.

- Identify strategies to try.

- Meet with parents for partnering conversation, if needed.

- Refer the child for additional supports, if needed.

Siva and Mateo: Putting It All Together

Kate and Joan were teachers in an inclusive classroom with children between ages three and five. On a typical visit to their classroom, I saw a few children sitting at a table coloring, while two others were putting toy people into the house they built; another child was leaning on a pillow paging through a book, and three children at the sensory table were pushing loose parts (bolts, metal rings, and small colanders) through cornstarch and water. The biggest group was building a museum with blocks. They were discussing as much as they were building, deciding what was needed. One child, Mateo, headed over to draw and cut out hieroglyphs while another made a sarcophagus using a cardboard box.

Kate and Joan moved around like hummingbirds, talking with the children, joining when invited and then after a few minutes moving to another group. I noticed that both teachers changed their interaction style depending on the children they were with. Kate colored and talked to the children at the table before walking a doll over to the house and knocking on the door. Joan silently watched the patterns as she swirled a bolt in the cornstarch until four-year-old Siva handed her a colander and said, "Use this." After a few minutes Joan went over to the museum to silently observe. Two of the children became guides and gave her a tour.

Kate and Joan were attuned to each child, engaging in individual ways of connecting. This happened through countless interactions and reflection on those interactions. They held morning meetings (circle time) where they sang songs and danced, guiding children through conflict resolution in which children worked through their own feelings while hearing other perspectives.

Kate and Joan had reflected on these experiences. They knew which children were attracted to messy materials and which children avoided them; which children gravitated toward loud, boisterous play; and which children sought quiet corners. They paid attention to the relationship skills each child showed as well as the diverse interests and experiences of the children.

Two of the children were Siva and Mateo. If these two interacted at all, it was usually Siva poking Mateo or trying to use a toy Mateo was holding. Mateo usually responded by yelling at Siva and walking away from him. Siva had difficulty focusing on a person talking to him and used few words in conversation. Kate and Joan had talked with Siva's parents about having him screened for sensory integration issues and helping him pick up on social cues. Reflecting on these two children gave the educators some insight.

Personal space

Siva tended to stand or sit less than a foot away from the person he was interacting with, closer than typical for the other children. The educators weren't sure if this was cultural or personal, but they kept this variable in mind. It could lead to conflicts with other children, and they could help articulate this difference in personal space with children in the moment. Meanwhile, Mateo tended to position himself two to four feet away from the person he was interacting with, which helped explain the types of interactions these two had.

Sensory

Siva and Mateo seemed somewhat neutral with messy materials, playing occasionally with them, neither seeking nor avoiding them in general. Siva had a hard time focusing on someone talking to him. This seemed to be more difficult when the noise level was louder. Mateo did not react differently to noise and was willing to play with children who got loud during play.

Relationship skills

Siva often watched children play before walking over to them and poking them, usually resulting in the other child pushing or yelling. During the conflict resolution process after a recent incident, Kate asked Siva if he wanted to play with the other child and he said yes. Kate told this to Joan during one of their reflections. They decided to try to notice when Siva typically poked others and try to model joining play before this happened.

Mateo often played with several children. He often was the leader in this group play, and he sometimes negotiated to include ideas of others. Other times, if another child insisted on their ideas being included, Mateo simply quit the game and played elsewhere. This happened most often with children who didn't understand his ideas, either due to lack of experience or cognitive development. Kate and Joan tried to find times when they could help Mateo understand the other child's point of view and help him articulate his ideas in a way the other child would understand, perhaps giving some background on the movie or book his game was based on.

Putting it all together

One day I came into the classroom to see Mateo leading four other children in a game where they pretended to sleep while Mateo hid some glass beads. Then he told them to "wake up" and look for the glass beads. Siva arrived late that morning. After greeting Kate and Joan, he watched the children playing this game. As one of the children walked by him in search of the glass beads, Siva poked him with a small plastic toy.

Kate was nearby and softly put a hand on Siva's shoulder, saying, "Do you want to play with them?" He told her he did, and she said, "Let's go find out what the rules are." She led him over to where the others were getting ready to start another round. She held Siva's hand and asked Mateo, "Can you tell me the rules, and I will show Siva?"

Mateo spoke quickly, "First they go to sleep and then—." Kate interrupted, "What does that look like? What do they do when they go to sleep?" Mateo said they close their eyes. Kate gave Siva's hand a gentle squeeze and told him, "We lay down and close our eyes." She held his hand as they lay down. He lay against Kate. She asked what happens next.

Mateo said, "Everybody wakes up and looks for the beads." Kate clarified, "So we open our eyes when we wake up?" Mateo agreed. Kate then gently squeezed Siva's hand and said, "Mateo will tell us to wake up, and then we open our eyes and look for the beads." Kate turned to Mateo and asked if they could try it.

Mateo told everyone to go to sleep. Still holding Siva's hand, Kate said, "OK, we close our eyes." She reminded Siva to keep his eyes closed while Mateo hid the beads. Then Mateo told everyone to wake up. Kate told Siva and then let go of his hand. Siva followed the other children as they walked around looking for beads. Kate was a few feet behind him. After a minute, she asked Siva if he remembered what the glass beads look like. He said he did, and she asked, "Do you think there are beads in this dollhouse?" Siva looked and didn't find any. Kate said, "No beads? That's OK. Where could we look next?" Siva went to a basket and looked. Kate followed silently behind, seeing that Siva seemed to remember the rules and was on task. She stopped following him.

After all the beads were found, Siva went over and closed his eyes with the others. Kate was interacting with other children but looked over every minute or so and saw that Siva was engaged in the game. On the third round, he found two beads.

In this story, Kate built a bridge between Mateo and the game he was leading and Siva, who wanted to join. She was attuned to the needs of both, asking Mateo to be more concrete going over the rules and holding Siva's hand to help him focus while she restated the rules. She was able to do this because she had reflected on these two children, identifying their strengths, preferences, and needs. In addition, Kate's interactions strengthened her relationships with both of these children. Interacting with the children as partners allows educators to form closer, more trusting relationships. Reflection on these interactions allows the educator to assess any barriers the child might experience in the classroom (such as sensory stimulus), and to develop ideas for bridges the child might need help with to interact with others.

Siva had no diagnosis, but there were signs that he perhaps had some sensory issues around sound that made it hard for him to engage. He also had some challenges with relationship skills that could point to other issues. While there was the possibility that he would pick up these skills a little later than others, Kate and Joan have worked with enough other children that they wondered whether there was an opportunity for more support. A developmental pediatrician would mostly likely screen Siva and would be interested in the way Siva pokes others to initiate interactions. Kate and Joan planned a partnering conversation with the parents. This story was a good reflection on how Siva could interact with others in the classroom. Even if he eventually qualified for other services, he would most likely stay in this classroom. The teachers removed barriers, created bridges, and fostered a sense of belonging.

The Biggest Barrier

I have addressed removing multiple barriers in the classroom so that all children are included. The biggest barrier, however, is our lack of imagination. In some ways, we have come a long way. Not too long ago, disabled children were excluded, not just from "mainstream" education but from most parts of society. Barrier after barrier has come down, thanks to activists confronting those in power who said that change was impossible. And each time, the voices of the disabled could not be ignored.

The changes that have happened were beneficial not only for the disabled but for all of society. As Tom Shakespeare points out in *Disability: The Basics*, everyone will experience disability at some point in their life. In the same way, inclusive early learning programs are good for everyone. When educators intentionally include disabled children, they open themselves up to including those who may not have a diagnosis but who struggle as our system becomes more standardized.

At each step, activists have led the way, showing us what we as a society are capable of. While disabled voices have played some part in shaping inclusive education, there have been far too many opportunities missed in creating programs. If we are to continue to move forward, we need more disabled educators in our field. And we need to listen to the voices of disabled adults about their experiences in schools. We need to include multiple experts in deciding what more we can do for the children in our care.

At the same time, we also need to include children and families of all cultures. We need to question what we mean by "typical" when we think of the development of a "typical" child. We need to recognize that our classrooms reflect the culture of the educators and can shut out other cultures unless we are intentional in recognizing our own cultural perspective and its influence on classroom expectations. And the field of early learning needs to recognize BIPOC care providers as cultural experts. How much would our field change if academics studied the practices of these educators as much as the lab schools associated with colleges and universities?

I am not trying to imply one type of program is better than another but rather to acknowledge that we have shone a light on only a small sample of our profession. We need to hold up the voices of BIPOC and disabled educators, parents, and children to learn ways to be more inclusive. The test is not whether we as educators have followed current inclusion practices but whether all the children feel a sense of belonging. We don't get to decide if we include everyone.

I hope that this book has been fair to those voices. While I can learn from people with various disabilities and cultures, I am speaking from my experience as a white, nondisabled educator who has reflected on my work with children of diverse strengths, preferences, needs, and cultures. I hope I continue to learn. I hope this book is a bridge to a world where inclusion is not a specialty but a reality in all programs and classrooms.

Glossary

While each of these terms may have multiple definitions, this is how I use the words in this book.

ableism: the devaluation and disregard for disabled people that results in societal attitudes that it is preferable for disabled people to do things the same way as nondisabled people

attunement: recognizing another person's emotional state and adapting one's own response in accordance, adjusting back and forth until the response seems appropriate

co-regulation: a nurturing adult sharing space and relationship with a dysregulated child in order to work toward soothing and regulating their physical and emotional state

cultural disconnect: miscommunication based on differing cultural perspectives

dysregulation: an imbalance in the body, when a child is having difficulty managing and adapting to stimuli in their environment, often resulting in a fight/flight/freeze response and difficulty in being rational

guidelines: similar to rules but are worded positively and are more general

heavy work: any activity that pushes or pulls against the body, such as carrying heavy items, pushing something heavy, or jumping

implicit bias: attitudes or stereotypes that affect our understanding, actions, and decisions in an unconscious way

Individualized Education Program (also known as Individual Education Plan or IEP): a plan legally required for all children who receive special education services in the United States that identifies the adaptations or related services the student needs

neurodivergence: the term used when brain function is different than the perceived norm, mostly referring to autism or ADHD

neurodiversity: the recognition that there are multiple ways people's brains process, learn, or behave

neurotypical: the term used when brain function is the same as the perceived norm. I often use this term to acknowledge neurodiversity and recognize that classroom environments and the norms of early childhood have been created by neurotypical people with their own cognitive needs in mind.

racism: the devaluation and disregard for Black, Indigenous, and people of color (BIPOC) that results in societal attitudes that it is preferable for BIPOC people to do things the same way as white people

regulation: when a child has the appropriate arousal level to meet current demands, managing and adapting to stimuli in their environment

sensory profile: the sensory input required to keep one's body in a well-regulated state

sensory stimulus: stimulus that is perceived by one of the seven senses: auditory (hearing), visual (seeing), tactile (feeling), oral (tasting and smelling), proprioceptive, vestibular, and interoceptive

temperament: a way to describe the differences in children's behavior, often sorted into easy, difficult, and slow to warm up. These categories can be helpful to remind educators that children will have different emotional responses to the same event or situations. While it can be a shorthand to help educators anticipate children's reactions, temperament describes tendencies, not a universal condition. No individual is universally "slow to warm up" or "flexible" in every situation.

References

Applewick, Megan. 2021. Interview with the author, June 10, 2021.

Bishop, Rudine Sims. 1990. "Mirrors, Windows, and Sliding Glass Doors." *Perspectives: Choosing and Using Books for the Classroom* 6, no. 3 (Summer): 9–11. https://scenicregional.org/wp-content /uploads/2017/08/Mirrors-Windows-and-Sliding-Glass-Doors.pdf.

Brown, Elizabeth Levine, Colleen K. Vesley, and Laura Dallman. 2016. "Unpacking Biases: Developing Cultural Humility in Early Childhood and Elementary Teacher Candidates." *Teacher Educators' Journal* 9 (Spring): 75–96. Retrieved from ERIC files: https://files.eric.ed.gov/fulltext/EJ1095643.pdf.

Brown, Lydia X. Z. 2011. "Identity and Hypocrisy: A Second Argument Against Person-First Language." Autistic Hoya, November 28, 2011. www.autistichoya.com/2011/11 /identity-and-hypocrisy-second-argument.html.

Brown, Stuart. 2017. "The Science of Play: Why Play?" PlayCore, September 20, 2017. www.playcore.com/news/why-play.

Chaves, Jamie, and Ashley Taylor. 2021. *The Why Behind Classroom Behaviors, PreK–5: Integrative Strategies for Learning, Regulation, and Relationships.* Thousand Oaks, CA: Corwin.

Collier, Roger. 2012. "Person-First Language: Noble Intent but to What Effect?" *Canadian Medical Association Journal* 184, no. 18 (December 11): 1977–8. https://doi.org/10.1503/cmaj.109-4319.

Connor, David J. 2011. "Questioning 'Normal': Seeing Children First and Labels Second." *School Talk: National Council of Teachers of English* 16, no. 2 (January): 1–3.

Derman-Sparks, Louise, and the A.B.C. Task Force. 1989. *Anti-Bias Curriculum: Tools for Empowering Young Children.* Washington, DC: National Association for the Education of Young Children.

Derman-Sparks, Louise, Julie Olsen Edwards, and Catherine M. Goins. 2020. *Anti-Bias Education for Young Children and Ourselves*, 2nd ed. Washington, DC: National Association for the Education of Young Children.

Evans, Betsy. 2000. *A Problem Solving Approach to Conflict* (video). Ypsilanti, MI: HighScope Press.

Evans, Betsy. 2016. *You Can't Come to My Birthday Party! Conflict Resolution with Young Children*, 2nd ed. Ypsilanti, MI: HighScope Press.

Fincham, Emmanuelle N., and Amanda R. Fellner. 2019. "Including Autism: Confronting Inequitable Practices in a Toddler Classroom." In *Promise in Infant-Toddler Care and Education. Occasional Paper Series* 2019, no. 42, article 7.

Freshman, Brenda. 2016. "Cultural Competency—Best Intentions Are Not Good Enough." *Diversity and Equality in Health and Care* 13 (3): 240–44.

Gartrell, Dan. 2012. *Education for a Civil Society: How Guidance Teaches Young Children Democratic Life Skills.* Washington, DC: National Association for the Education of Young Children.

Gilliam, Walter S. 2005. *Prekindergartners Left Behind: Expulsion Rates in State Prekindergarten Programs.* FCD Policy Brief Series no. 3, May 2005. New York: Foundation for Child Development.

Greene-Moton, Ella, and Meredith Minkler. 2020. "Cultural Competence or Cultural Humility? Moving Beyond the Debate." *Health Promotion Practice* 21, no. 1 (January 1): 142–45. https://doi.org/ 10.1177/1524839919884912.

Hall, Edward T. 1976. *Beyond Culture*. New York: Anchor Books.

Haynes-Mendez, Kelley, and Jill Engelsmeier. 2020. "Cultivating Cultural Humility in Education." Childhood Education Innovations 96 (3): 22–29. Childhood Education International: Washington, DC.

Hehir, Thomas. 2005. *New Directions in Special Education: Eliminating Ableism in Policy and Practice*. Cambridge, MA: Harvard Education Press.

Huber, Mike. 2017. *Embracing Rough-and-Tumble Play: Teaching with the Body in Mind*. St. Paul, MN: Redleaf Press.

Huber, Mike, and Liz Nelson. 2021. "Developing Our Sensory Systems Through Exploration." St. David's Center. April 1, 2021. www.stdavidscenter.org/article/developing-our-sensory-systems -through-exploration.

Langworthy, Sara E. 2015. *Bridging the Relationship Gap: Connecting with Children Facing Adversity*. St. Paul, MN: Redleaf Press.

Liebowitz, Cara. 2015. "I Am Disabled: On Identity-First Versus People-First Language." The Body Is Not an Apology, March 20, 2015. https://thebodyisnotanapology.com/magazine /i-am-disabled-on-identity-first-versus-people-first-language.

National Association for the Education of Young Children. 2020. *Developmentally Appropriate Practice (DAP) Position Statement*. Washington, DC: NAEYC. www.naeyc.org/sites/default/files /globally-shared/downloads/PDFs/resources/position-statements /dap-statement_0.pdf.

Oliver, Mike. 1990. *The Individual and Social Models of Disability*. Paper presented at the Joint Workshop of the Living Options Group and the Research Unit of the Royal College of Physicians, July 23, 1990. https://disability-studies.leeds.ac.uk/wp-content/uploads/sites/40 /library/Oliver-in-soc-dis.pdf.

Pastel, Encian, Katie Steele, Julie Nicholson, Cyndi Maurer, Julia Hennock, Jonathan Julian, Tess Unger, and Nathanael Flynn. 2019. *Supporting Gender Diversity in Early Childhood Classrooms: A Practical Guide.* London: Jessica Kingsley Publishers.

Perry, Bruce D. 2020. "Regulate, Relate, Reason (Sequence of Engagement)." *Neurosequential Network Stress & Trauma Series.* Info NMN. Upload date April 2, 2020, YouTube video, 18:25. www.youtube.com/watch?v=LNuxy7FxEVk.

Recchia, Susan L., and Yoon-Joo Lee. 2013. *Inclusion in the Early Childhood Classroom: What Makes a Difference?* New York: Teachers College Press.

Roffman, Leslie, Todd Wanerman, and Cassandra Britton. 2011. *Including One, Including All: A Guide to Relationship-Based Early Childhood Inclusion.* St. Paul, MN: Redleaf Press.

Shakespeare, Tom. 2018. *Disability: The Basics.* New York: Routledge.

Smith, Greg. 2001. "Backtalk: The Brother in a Wheelchair." *Essence* 6 (July 20): 162.

Statman-Weil, Katie. 2020. *Trauma-Responsive Strategies for Early Childhood.* St. Paul, MN: Redleaf Press.

Tervalon, Melanie, and Jann Murray-Garcia. 1998. "Cultural Humility Versus Cultural Competence: A Critical Distinction in Defining Physician Training Outcomes in Multicultural Education." *Journal of Heatlh Care for the Poor and Underserved* 9, no. 2 (May): 117–25. https://doi.org/ 10.1353/hpu.2010.0233.

White, Kari. 2021. Interview with the author, May 12, 2021.

Wymer, Sarah C., Amanda P. Williford, and Ann S. Lhospital. 2020. "Exclusionary Discipline Practices in Early Childhood." *Young Children* 75, no. 3 (July): 36–44.

Index